The Sermon's Over

To: Darlene
Good
Luck
God
Bless

Rev.
John
Motley
III

4/90

Reverend John W. Motley, III

After The Sermon's Over

Reverend John W. Motley, III

Copyright © 1997
All Rights Reserved

ISBN 1-55630-507-9

PUBLISHED BY:
BRENTWOOD CHRISTIAN PRESS
4000 BEALLWOOD AVENUE
COLUMBUS, GEORGIA 31904

Dedication

To my mother, Mrs. Cornelia Williams, my brother, James Keith Motley, My three younger sisters, Mrs. Kimberly Phillips, Julie Motley, and Lesia Motley. Also to my children, Sean Louis Motley and Imani Cornelia Motley.

To the congregation of the First Baptist Church of W. Mifflin, Pennsylvania, my pastor, George A. Williams.

My Friends, associates, and all others who have been influential in my life and the ministry that has become my life.

Together we have seen, lived, and enjoyed the messages and the promises contained in this book.

Finally I want to thank Mrs. Donna Hilliard, for the art work, my mother-in-law Mrs. Mildred Rue, for the proofreading, and Mrs. Carol Antozak, for the word processing.

May God continue to bless us all.

Rev. John W. Motley, III

Acknowledgements

I am indeed grateful to my wife, Vicki, who has worked with me in every phase of my life and in this ministry. She is much more than just a wife, she is an extension of myself and has given unselfishly of her time and talents, and has supported me in every way humanly possible.

She joins with me in the prayer that all people that read this book, whether minister, layman, or parishioner, that God will open up to you the meaning of the scriptures and the purpose for which this book was written, will be revealed to you also.

God bless you all.

Introduction

How many times have you thought after attending a church service and heard the Word of God proclaimed from the pulpit, how much more you could gain from the message, if you were actually able to read the text?

Many people have attended church all of their lives and have even thought they have gone to church with an open mind and heart, and have left church with only a portion of the message. The preparation of a delivered text is a difficult job that requires prayer and much study, to show thyself approved unto God, a workman that needeth not be ashamed, rightly dividing the word of truth. Sometimes even though the minister has studied diligently, the Holy Spirit leads in a different direction, when the actual text is being delivered. Notes, points of reference and scripture notes are often put back into the briefcase for future use. Always in study, you find things that you did not know before, whereby making you better off for having done the added research and better prepared when you deliver it to the congregation.

It is good to hear a speech delivered to you, but none can argue the fact that when you have an opportunity to read it for yourself, it takes on new meaning! That is the purpose of this book. It allows the children of God who are seeking a further understanding of the Word, or a minister who is researching a particular text, the opportunity to see how someone else presented it.

It also gives you the advantage that when you are dealing with situations in your life, you can read for yourself what God says about the situation through, the inspired word that He delivered to His preacher to deliver to his people. I have never preached a sermon that I did not feel that God had given to me, which makes this also an invaluable treasure of heavenly instruction, because I gave the message God designed for that particular congregation.

I sincerely pray that you will be blessed by it's contents and find many uses for the materials preserved and collected herein.

What is a sermon? A sermon is a speech given as instruction in religion or morals, usually delivered by a clergyman, using a text from scripture.

How can reading one help me? It will help because you can read it whenever you like, as often as you like, research it for yourself, and be sure that you understand completely the instruction given in the discourse. When it comes to salvation, it is important that we understand what we hear and prove all things by additional study.

Contents

Part I: Sermons

Part II: Research and Study

Part I
Sermons

Is God Still Resting?

First of all, I give honor to God, to all the clergy, officers and members of First Baptist Church, and all of my family and friends: I would like to say it is good to see you all here this evening, etc.

What we're going to talk about is a message that God laid on my heart when I first decided to accept the call. God said in Jeremiah, "Thou shalt go to all that I shall send thee, and whatsoever I command thee thou shalt speak." So I'm going to ask the question --

Is God Still Resting?

Genesis 2:1-2 states, *Thus the heavens and the earth were finished, and all the host of them. And on the seventh day God ended His work which He had made; and He rested on the seventh day from all of His work He had made."* God rested! That's probably why a lot of us think we can get away with or do anything we want to on Sunday or any other day. We figure God won't know anyway, He's probably tired and taking a nap from watching all those other folks, in those other churches! Am I right about it? AMEN. What we have to consider is that in Genesis, God was not resting as we know it in a physical sense. We should not conceive of God's rest on the seventh day as necessary because of sheer exhaustion after his six days of creative work. The verb in this case means to cease and desist from work. To say that God rested is a description of God's activity in terms conducive to man's understanding. In other words, putting it down on man's level, not on God's level! The omnipotent God who fainteth not, neither is weary...(Isaiah 40:28), did not cease from his labors on the seventh day just because he needed a rest. God couldn't rest if he could rest, with all of us down here.

I know we all remember as children or young adults, when we used to wait until we thought our parents were asleep to do things that we knew we weren't supposed to do. I know we all can relate to that. For instance: If our parents told us not to touch a certain thing in the house or not to eat a certain thing in the house, no matter how many other freedoms we had, we couldn't wait until they went to bed or were resting, and we'd do it anyway! Sometimes we as adults are guilty of the same thing, when we think nobody's looking. This is my house, and none of the folks at the church have anything to do with what I do here. AMEN. So, it was also in the Bible days. People had to keep watch because the other tribes would attack when they thought you were asleep or resting. They just went in and attacked, and worried about paying the price later, even if the people weren't asleep and they got caught. So, it was also in the beginning when God placed Adam and Eve in the garden. He gave them charge of, and placed them over everything in the garden. But, God placed one restriction. He said of all the trees of the garden, thou mayest freely eat, but, the Tree of Knowledge, of good and evil, thou shalt not eat. They had complete freedom in the garden only restricted by one prohibition. But, what happened? The serpent approached first Eve and said, *"Do you really mean to tell me that God said you're not supposed to eat from all of them?"* Well, that's not what God meant. And Eve probably said that God has given us all of this. We have all we want to eat; hang around this pretty garden all day; we have power and authority over everything; we're in charge. And besides that, he said if we eat the fruit we're going to die. The devil said that's not what he meant by that. That fruit is probably good too! As we all know, things aren't much different today. Someone's always trying to distort and turn around something that God said. *This reminds me of a story about a certain school teacher that played a game to try to determine what children would be when they grew up, by changing the numbers in their age. For instance, she would say, "Johnny, how old are you?" He would say, "I'm 13." She would say, "That's good, a one and a three." If you change that around, that would be 31. By the time you are 31 you should be through high school, college and working, with a wife and children. She*

14

would do that with each student, until finally she got to Billy and said, "Little Billy, tell me how old you are so we can tell you how you'll turn out." Little Billy said, "I'm eleven. Let's see you mess with that!" That's the way it is with God. You can try to change God's word around all you want, but it still remains the same, no matter how you look at it. You know the rest of the story. Eve gave some of the fruit to Adam. They both ate it. Their eyes were opened. They realized that they had sinned and ran and hid from God. You can run, but, you cannot hide. God called them out and they confessed. He kicked them out of the garden! We've been trying to sneak behind God's back ever since.

Moving on to Adam's son Cain, who slew his brother Abel, when he thought God was resting and asked, *"Am I my brother's keeper?"* It came to pass that man's sins became worse and worse, trying to get away with all that they could. But, Noah knew that God wasn't resting. Noah remained faithful, or I wouldn't be here today to tell the story! Surely, Daniel knew God wasn't resting when he was in the lion's den. As we move on again, we find the children of Israel in bondage in Egypt. But, God was still on the job. He sent Moses to deliver them from bondage. And, we all know that Moses didn't get any rest. He couldn't even go up into the mountains to talk with God before the people started sinning again! God was not resting. He gave the people a song to sing so that while they were working they would be reminded of how good God had been and how He always delivered them when they were in trouble. And in case you're wondering what song they sang you CAN find it in Deuteronomy 32:1. Maybe if it were us today, we'd be singing, "Because he lives, I can face tomorrow. Because He lives, all fear is gone. Because I know Ho holds the future, and life is worth living, just because He lives." Or maybe you would sing, "Oh, they tell me of a home, far, far away. Oh, they tell me of a home far beyond the skies. Oh, they tell me of a home where no storm clouds rise. Oh, they tell me of an uncloudy day. Oh, they tell me of a King and His beauty there. And, they tell me that my eyes shall behold where He sits on the throne. That it is whiter than snow. In a city that is made of gold. Oh, they tell me of an uncloudy day!"

Is God Still Resting?

Surely, Job knew that God wasn't resting when he said I know that thou can do everything, and that no thought can be withheld from thee. In Ezekiel's day, 25 priests thought God was resting and turned their backs to the church and started worshiping the sun. Can you believe that 25 priests, called out, set apart and separate, worshipping the sun, a creation of God; not worshiping the Creator, but that which was created! These men were in God's service. I know a lot of us can relate to that. You have a car that you do not want anyone to ride in. You go out and wax it all day. You have dishes that you only use for special occasions and that might only come once a year. You have clothes that you are saving. They are even too precious to put on. Waiting for that one day that you can go out and finally wear them! I don't want to seem hard, but I'm going to tell you something: Tomorrow may never come. Nobody is promised tomorrow. So, you better get out there and enjoy life and enjoy what God has blessed you with. And, start worshiping the Creator, not the creations! Am I right about it? People here do not act like that!

Anyway, <u>GOD</u> <u>WAS</u> <u>STILL</u> <u>ON</u> <u>THE</u> <u>JOB.</u> He was not resting. The sins of the people were so bad that God got up and left his own house in the temple. Can you imagine that? They were sinning so bad that he just couldn't take it. He got up and left. But, on the way out the door he gave his angels charge to destroy the city, starting at the church, the 25 priests and so on.

Things were getting bad and the righteous people were starting to wonder what was going to happen next? World situations had gotten out of hand. But, God was not resting. He sent his son Jesus. Our Rock, Our Sword, Our Shield. "The Lily of the Valley, The Bright and Morning Star. The wheel in the middle of the wheel. No one in the history of creation has been like JESUS. No other name had so much power. No other name *has* so much power. Adam couldn't take care of the garden well enough. Abel

16

couldn't raise sheep fat enough. Noah couldn't build the Ark fast enough. Abraham wasn't faithful enough. Joseph didn't rule Egypt long enough. Moses didn't lead the people through the desert good enough. Daniel didn't pray hard enough. Gideon didn't fight hard enough. Samson wasn't strong enough. David didn't kill giants quick enough. David didn't write songs sweet enough. David wasn't King enough. Job didn't have patience enough. Jeremiah didn't preach convincingly enough. Ezekiel didn't have visions enough. Ezekiel didn't preach to the dry bones long enough! Jonah didn't cry out of the whale loud enough. Malachi didn't collect the tithes long enough. John the Baptist didn't Baptlze the people **well** enough, but he pointed everybody to Jesus!

There is no other name by which you can be saved. Jesus will take you no matter what kind of condition you're in. He'll reach all the way down in the muck and mire. He will pick you up. He'll pull you out. He'll clean you up. And, he'll give you a new song to sing! Jesus can heal your body. He can save you soul. Jesus is real. I know it. He healed me. When I was sick; when I was afflicted; when I was down and out, he gave me a song to sing! When I had diabetes and the doctor told me I might not survive and that I was the worst case in the history of the hospital, I got down on my hands and knees and I cried out to the God of Heaven and I said, *"Jesus save me. I don't want to be a diabetic."* Then, He reached down and touched me and He healed me, and He gave me a new song to sing. I know that Jesus is real. He wakes me up in the morning. I talk to him everyday. He goes with me through my day. He handles all my troubles, and He puts me to bed at night.

Do you know Jesus? Do you know Jesus?

Has He touched you? Has He healed you? Can you reach out and touch? Do you know that somebody's watching you? Do you know that you don't have to be burden laden? Do you know that you don't have to go through life's afflictions? Do you know that there's peace on the top of the hill? Do you know that the only thing you have to do is trust and believe and keep your eye on the prize which is Jesus Christ our Lord and Savior? The **lily of the valley**.

Do you know that Jesus can save you today? Do you know Jesus? God is not resting. Jesus is not resting. He still continues to heal us today. He still continues to talk with us today. Satan might tempt you today. But, that's his job. We go to ours! Like the old people say, "As long as he keeps barking at you on the outside, the faster it makes you run to Jesus." Do you know Jesus? Do you know Him? You better get to know Him. Besides being a good friend, He's a healer; He's our Savior! As it says in John 1:1-3 In the beginning was the word and the word was God and the word was with God. All things were created by Him. Which means that Jesus can do anything. He has power over everything. We're all His creation. Do you know Him? God's not resting. *HE'S JUST WAITING.*

January 31, 1985

Are We Still About Our Father's Business?

Luke 2:46-49

And it came to pass that after three days, they found him in the temple sitting in the midst of the doctors, both hearing them and asking them questions. And all that heard him were astonished at his understanding and the answers. And when they saw him they were amazed. And his mother said unto him, Son, why hadst thou thus dealt with us? Behold thy Father and I have sought thee sorrowing. And he said unto them, *"How is it that ye sought me? Wist ye not that I must be about my Father's business?"*

Now, some churches and church people took Jesus literally. They have turned their churches into big businesses or huge marketing conglomerates. They play bingo in the church; have raffles in the church. Some churches you have to fight through all the church auxiliaries waving tickets at you or selling something, to get to your seat in the pews! Some of our churches even have lotteries. You can go to some churches and get everything you're not supposed to get and nothing you need to get! Churches even try to play keep-up with the Jone's, too. We want what Second Baptist has or what the big churches have. If they don't have Jesus, we shouldn't want anything they have. *Are we still about our Father's business?*

Here's something that is amusing to me. A lot of our churches are becoming franchises like McDonalds or Kentucky Fried Chicken. You see them all over the country. You know Kentucky Fried Chicken wherever you see one, because it has the Colonel's picture all over the place, but he's not there. That's the same way with some of our churches. Their big beautiful crosses are all over the place and big life-size pictures of Jesus hanging from the ceilings, but, He's not there. He's tragically absent! They're just using his name the way the chicken folks use the Colonel's name! Am I right about it? AMEN. But regardless of

19

what we do with Jesus, He's still number in Heaven. It doesn't matter whether we accept him or reflect him. But, it should matter to us. God wants us all to be saved. But, if you refuse to receive him, he won't knock you down and drag you in. He said whosoever will, let him come. Jesus is still number 1 in Heaven and if we want to be truly blessed, we ought to make him number 1 in our lives. *Are we still about our Father's business?* Or is the church just another franchise?

Paul said, "He is before all things and by him all things consist. The word before not only speaks of his pre-existence, but also of his preeminence! John said, "That which from the beginning which we have heard, which we have seen with our eyes, which we have looked upon and our hands have handled of the word of life. For the life was manifested, and we have seen it, and to bear witness and to show unto you the eternal life that was with the Father, and was manifest unto us." Then John broke it down and said, "In the beginning was the word, and the word was with God and the word was God. The same was in the beginning with God." In other words, when time began, Jesus was already in existence. Maybe we are teaching this in our churches or maybe we're not. Are we still about our Father's business? All through Jesus's entire life, he had the most trouble out of church folks and religious leaders. It seems that things haven't changed much. Have they?

What is the business of the church? Do we teach in our churches that if you're in sin you're in bondage? Or, if any of your possessions possess you, you are a slave? Especially if they become more important than Jesus. When what you've accumulated in life owns you; you're not free! When you have a house you can't enjoy, when you have a car you don't want anybody to touch, when you have clothes that you can't wear, except on special occasions, that only come once in a lifetime. When you have dishes that you can't use because they're too precious? I want you to know something. Tomorrow might not come! You better start enjoying life better, and use what God has given you and blessed you with. Stop worshiping that which was created

20

and start worshiping the Creator! Don't get wrapped up in things you have to leave behind! We have to teach church folks to get wrapped up, tied up, and tangled up in Jesus! When Jesus said that church folks got mad. You're not mad are you? Not if we're still about our Father's business! Did you know that sin will blind you? In the Bible days when things had gotten good, people even forgot that they were slaves in Egypt, and in bondage to the Romans and the Babylonians. But, all while Jesus was dealing with them, He still loved them. Much like our preachers today. Am I right about it? Do you realize that if Jesus did not love the sinner, all of us would be in HELL today! But, what of the business of the church today? Are we still in business?

The church in the theological word book of the Bible, states that the church is a building for church worship, or the Lord's house. Church also means an assembly of people. So, that means we are the church. The church is supposed to be composed of Christians. People who are supposed to have been baptized, believe that Jesus Christ is the Messiah, and ask for His forgiveness of sins. Paul referred to the Christian church as an assembly of God in Christ or the body of Christ. The church originated in the redemptive act of God in Christ and lives through its unity with Jesus in His death and resurrection and through the indwelling of the Holy Spirit. We have a responsibility. We have to constantly continue to build up the church. We have to tell folks about Jesus. He didn't tell us to keep it a secret! The church has to constantly educate the people. Sunday School, Prayer Meetings, Bible Study, and the Sunday Worship Service. These things all represent the church at study. People have to know that Jesus gave His life for us, that we may have life. People have to know that He healed the sick and is still healing today. People have to know that He walked on water and had control over nature. People have to know that He forgives sin. People have to know that upon this rock He has the keys to Heaven and Hell. People have to know that one day soon He will bind up the Devil for a thousand years. People have to know that He has all power. People have to know that He said suffer the little children to

21

come unto me, because such as these will inherit the Kingdom of Heaven. People ought to know that He said I knock at the door and wait and whosoever will let Him come. People ought to know that He is the bright and morning star. People ought to know that He's coming back again. Are we still about our Father's business? Or are we like the chicken folks?

Are we having church in church? Jesus is as real today as He was in Bible times. Are we teaching our children? A Christian church is a company of regenerate persons, baptized on profession of faith in Christ, united in covenant for worship, instruction, observance of Christian ordinances, and for such service as gospel requires; recognizing and accepting Christ as the supreme law giver and Lord, and taking the Bible as the divinely inspired word of God and therefore trustworthy, authoritative, and all sufficient rule of faith and practice. Are we up to the task? Have we done thus saith the Lord? Or are we just another franchise?

Who Do You Serve?

Joshua 24:14-15   1 Kings 18:21   Luke 16:13

Song:

Well, I woke up this morning with my mind-stayed on Jesus.
I woke up this morning with my mind on the Lo-rd,
I woke up this morning with my mind-stayed on Jesus,
Hallelu - Hallelu - Hallelujah! Repeat.

Now, therefore, fear the Lord, and serve him in sincerity and in truth. Put away the gods which your fathers served on the other side of the flood and in Egypt, and serve ye the Lord. And if it seems evil unto you to serve the Lord, choose you this day whom ye will serve, whether the gods that you fathers served that were on the other side of the flood, or the gods of the Amorites, in whose land ye dwell. But, as for me and my house, we will serve the Lord. 1 Kings 18:21 - And Elijah came unto the people and said, How long halt ye between two opinions? If the Lord be God, follow Him. But, if Baal, then follow him. And the people answered him not a word.

We live in a world today where anything that we want is at the tip of our fingers. Everything has been modernized, computerized, and homogenized. We have precooked meals, microwave ovens, and talking cars. Anything and everything that we could imagine can be easily obtainable. In America, we live like kings compared to the rest of the world because God has blessed us to live in this land, filled with milk and honey. We have slowly graduated from slavery times to good times. From poverty to liberty and prosperity. From down and out to a complete turn-about. We have forgotten about God! Much like the people in Joshua and Elijah's day, we have somehow pushed God in the background of our lives. We have put in front of Him, other gods. We have our pretty clothes that we put on; we have our fine automobiles that we stand around and wax all day; we wash them and shine them and dare someone to lean on them. Those pretty dishes at home in the closet, put aside for special occasions or when we want to impress some folks. Fine silver, so pretty that we don't even eat out of it unless the President's coming over for dinner. But, we forget all about God from whom all blessings flow. I've got a problem with that. If it were not for the Lord, we would not have anything. He wakes us up every morning, and gives us a reasonable portion of health and strength. He sets our feet upon the carpet and starts us on our way. He protects us while we are on our jobs and provides for us a means to take care of our wives, children, and our families. God protects us from all things seen and unseen. He brought us all the way from the plantation house to positions in the Senate, Congress, Supreme Court, and the White House. God has been good to us. But, we have not been good to God. Matt 6:24 says that you can't serve two masters. For either you will hate the one and love the other, or else you will hold to one and despise the other. You can't serve two masters. A songwriter said, "I will trust in the Lord, I will trust in the Lord, I will trust in the Lord until die." Another said, "Precious Lord, take my hand, lead me on, let me stand." Another got happy and said:

> "Amazing grace, how sweet the sound,
> That saved a wretch like me.
> I once was lost, but, now I'm found
> Was blind, but, now I see."

Many of us are blinded, not physically blinded, but spiritually blinded by our own selfishness and our own righteousness. Even though in the sight of God we are filthy as rags, no matter how good we think we're living. We take everything we do for granted. We turn the key and we expect the car to start. We hit the switch and we expect the light to come on, but, I'm here to tell you that without God you wouldn't be able to lift your body out of bed to get to the switch. Without God, you wouldn't be able to make the money to pay for the car, to put the key in and go wherever you want. Without God you would not be able to go to the job that makes you too tired to come to prayer meeting and to stingy to pay your tithes and offerings. We are going around robbing God of his time and spending his money. Whom do you serve? Ye cannot serve God and mammon (money) Much like Joshua who had gone through all of Canaan possessing all the land and overcoming every obstacle, trial, and tribulation, until he had possessed all that God had promised them, so, we also came all the way from the fields with a song in our hearts and dust in our pockets, trusting God and standing on his promises. Leaning on the everlasting arms. Whom do you serve? How long halt ye between two opinions was the question Elijah asked, as he addressed all of Judah and four hundred and fifty of Baal's prophets? The people were confused because they were in a strange land and they took a lot of things for granted. They had forgotten what their fathers had gone through before coming into the land which was to be their inheritance. Also Jezebel, King Ahab's wife, had had all the prophets of the Lord put to death and commanded all the people to worship Baal. Ahab was an evil Ring. He did more evil in the sight of the Lord than his father Omri. Ahab did more to provoke God than all the kings before him. To get his attention, God sent Elijah to tell the King that it would not rain for three years. Then, he told him to hide by a brook, and he had ravens to feed him there throughout the famine. He had bread in the morning and meat in the evening. He drank from the brook. After three years, the Lord told Elijah to go see the King and gather all the people of Israel on Mt. Carmel, and also, the prophets of Baal, to prove to the people who was the real God. This reminds me of a story about Elijah. He took twelve stones and rebuilt the altar of the Lord. He built a trench around it and put wood on it. Elijah cut the bullock in pieces, dressed it and lay it on the wood. He had the people get buckets of water and drench the sacrifice and the altar three times. The water overflowed and filled the trench. Then Elijah prayed and lightening came from Heaven and consumed the altar and the sacrifice.

Whom do you, serve?

Where Do We Go From Here?

Luke 22:39-43

And He came out and went, as He was wont, to the Mount of Olives; and His disciples also followed Him. And when He was at the place, He said unto them, "Pray that ye enter not into temptation." And He was withdrawn from them about a stones throw away and kneeled down and prayed, saying, "Father, if thou be willing, remove this cup from me; never the less, not my will but thine be done." And there appeared an angel from heaven strengthening Him. Where do we go from here? Sometimes we also get to that point in our lives when we have to make a decision about what direction our lives are going to. We think we have seen it all or have come to our fork in the road where we have to decide whether we are going to follow the crowd or do what we know is right even if we are the only person to go that way. You may be the only person to go that way. When we think of all the places we have been and all the experiences that we have had, and all the things we have done, and it feels like we have fulfilled our life's purposes, we should take time to reflect and ask ourselves: What next, or where do we go from here? It is very important, especially today to make the right decision. If the last four years didn't teach us that, the next four will! Blacks are confronted with a lot of choices. Our future in this world depends on every one of us making the right choice. Blacks have to make a choice to follow the "out" crowd, not the "in" crowd. You can't miss school and smoke pot and hang out in the clubs and end up on welfare, just because everybody else is doing it! If it is wrong, it is wrong, and just because everybody else is doing it, doesn't make it right. In the sixties, Blacks made a decision. We marched, sang, prayed, and united together to insure Civil Rights, while some others of us decided we wanted to be hippies, trying to be like our white counterparts who are

27

now heads of major corporations, while Blacks are still on welfare rolls and trying to get into job training programs. Be prepared. Rich white people's children could afford to grow their hair long and sit around in corners playing guitars and protesting against the draft. We have to decide to keep our jobs and our families together. We have to do what we know is right. A good example is John Thompson, Coach of the Georgetown Basketball Team. He is not popular with the media or a large majority of the people. But, he goes on and does what he thinks is right. He first built men, then basketball players, and ended up with the No. 1 team in the country! And no matter what they do after graduation, they'll go on to be better men in the future because of it. A lot of decisions that we make may not be the popular one, but, it may be the right one! Now the twelve disciples were faced with a tough decision. They had to leave their wives and families, and their jobs to follow Jesus. As a result, they traveled a lot of places with Jesus and witnessed a lot of miracles. In the beginning when Jesus was led by the Spirit into the wilderness to be tempted by the Devil, he fasted forty days and forty nights. Surely He must have thought, where do I go from here? But, His life was predestined. It was already worked out for him, far in advance. He was to go out and do a lot of great works. So, He went out saying, "Repent, for the Kingdom of God is at hand." He went into Galilee healing all manner of sickness among the people. Everywhere He went, He was followed by great multitudes of people from far and near. Seeing the multitudes, He went up into the mountains. And, when He was set, He must have asked the question. But, He called His disciples to Him and delivered the Sermon on the Mount. He taught them and said, "Rejoice and be exceedingly glad for great is your reward in Heaven." He even taught them to love their enemies. Where do we go from here? Jesus came down from the mountains and healed a leper and healed the centurions' servant, just by speaking the word! Then, they went on to Peter's house. His mother-in-law was sick with fever. He touched her and the fever immediately left her. Then, one of the disciples asked to go bury his father, but, Jesus said, "Let the dead bury their dead." Meaning let the spiritually dead bury the physically dead. Follow me. Where do we go from here?

Then, He entered into a ship and His disciples followed Him. Then, a great wave and storm arose and the ship tossed and turned, but, He was asleep. Then, one of His disciples went down and woke Him and said, "Lord, save us" or we won't go anywhere from here. Then, he arose and rebuked the winds and the storm ceased. When they got to the other side they found two men possessed by devils coming out of the tombs. Now, this is a perfect example of sins blight. These men had been cutting themselves, abusing themselves and terrorizing everyone in the countryside. The one man had the devil for a long time and wore no clothes. He was out of his mind. He had even been chained and he broke them. It must have been a horrible sight. There were so many of them in this man that they were called legion. But, Jesus rebuked them and cast them out into a herd of swine. Next, he cured a man, sick of palsy, brought to him on a bed. He said, "Son, be of good cheer. Thy sins be forgiven thee. Arise, take up thy bed and walk and go into thy own house." He was healed.

Where do we go from here? Next, there was a woman who had been sick with a blood disease for 12 years. She came up behind Him and reached out and touched the hem of his garment. He turned around and said, "Daughter, be of good comfort. Thy faith has made thee whole." Moving on, He raised Jarius' daughter from the dead, cured two blind men, and went into all the villages teaching the word. Where do we go from here? He called his disciples unto Him and gave power over demons and to heal the sick and all manner of diseases. He, then sent them out into the lost sheep of Israel saying, "He that receiveth you, receiveth me." He, then went on to rebuke the Pharisees and told His parables. He fed five thousand people with five loaves of bread and two fishes, and even had leftovers! He even walked on water and invited Peter in for a walk. But, Peter was scared and started to sink, and cried out and Jesus saved him. Where do we go from here? Then, Jesus went on to have a conversation with

29

Moses and Elias, or as we might say it, "Had a little rap session with the boys," just checking to see how things were still going in Heaven. The disciples then saw God appear in a cloud saying, "This is my beloved Son, in whom I am well pleased. Hear ye Him." Jesus went on to pray with the children, healed two more blind men, and even cursed a fig tree. Where do we go from here? He, then instituted the Lord's Supper. He took the bread and blessed it and divided it up among His disciples saying, "This is my body which is broken for you." Likewise with the wine he said, "This is the blood of the New Testament which was shed for you." And, when they had sung a song they went out into the Mount of Olives. Where do we go from here? We know the rest of the story. Or as Martin Luther King said, "I've been to the mountain top, and I've seen the promised land. I'm not fearing any man, because my eyes have seen the glory of the coming of the Lord. I have a dream." Or, as the Apostle Paul said, "But, watch thou in all things." Endure afflictions. Do the work of the evangelist. Make foolproof of thy ministry. (Jesus) For I am now ready to be offered, and the time of departure is at hand. I have fought a good fight, I have kept the faith, I have finished my course. Soon afterward, Jesus was betrayed and brought before Pilate, sentenced and crucified. Then, Joseph of Arimathea, claimed the body from Pilate, put Him in clean garments, and laid Him in a new tomb. By then, all of the women who had been ministering unto Jesus and all the disciples had to be asking, "Where do we go from here?" But, on the third day, Jesus got up and rolled the stone away and walked among men!

Jesus, then sent His disciples out in the world saying, "Tell them that I am alive, and still answer prayer; tell them that I still heal the sick; tell them that there is only one name under the sun by which they can be saved; tell them that I am the one called wonderful; tell them that they don't have to be burdened, ladened, or afflicted; tell them that their time has come; tell them that I am their rock, their sword, their shield, the lily of the valley, the bright and morning star, the wheel in the middle of the wheel. Tell them that I laid down my life, that they may have eternal life, and have it abundantly. Tell them that somebody is watching them; tell them that it is not good to be physically alive, but spiritually dead; tell them all they have to do is trust and believe and keep their eye on the prize; tell them that I was in the beginning and likewise in the end; tell them that I am the Prince of Peace, Lord of lords, King of Kings; tell them that if they have a prayer they ought to pray a song, they ought to sing it. Tell them that before Abraham was, I am. Tell them that if they deny me now, I will deny them in front of my Father; tell them that I am coming back again."

Do you know what Jesus is saying? He isn't going to beg you for your salvation. Are you ready to accept Christ as your personal Savior? I did. He said, "Whosoever will let Him come." He's not going to beat you up, knock you down and drag you in. It's up to you. He said, "I come to the door and knock and whosoever receives me, will have everlasting life." Where do you go from here?

Black History Day Service
January 1993

What Is This?

Acts 2:1-4, 12

And when the day of Pentecost was fully come, they were all in one place and in one accord. And suddenly, there came a sound from Heaven, as of a rushing mighty wind, and it filled all the house where they were sitting. And there, appeared unto them, cloven tongues, like as of fire, and it sat upon each of them. And they were all filled with the Holy Ghost, and began to speak in other tongues, as the Spirit gave them utterance. And they were amazed and were in doubt, saying one to another, "What meaneth this?" Or, if you will - What is this? To find out what it is, we have to go back. First of all, in our own lives, I know we can all remember times when we have seen things that were so spectacular that it had us spellbound. It was so new, but so different, because no one had ever seen it or heard it before. It was a new experience. When we see these type of things, we often are amazed at the effect or the visible part, but we know there's something more to it. People were shocked and amazed at the first telephone, the first radio, the first automobile, and the first television set. Also, the first boat, submarine, airplane, and now the first space shuttle. The whole world was devastated by the first atomic bomb. We had never witnessed such power! We knew the effect, or what it did, but we knew something made it do what it did. We see what it does which is the obvious. But, HOW does it do it? In other words, What is This?

Before we look at what it is, let's look at what it can do. After receiving the Holy Spirit, Peter and John went out preaching the word. They saved three thousand souls and added to the church on Peter's first sermon. Then, Peter and John went up to the temple to pray and they encountered a man who had been lame all of his life from his mother's womb. He was taken daily to the church and lay daily at the gate of the temple which was called Beautiful. Now, it was called Beautiful not because of the folks inside, but because the gates were made of Corinthian Gold. Now, he was there daily so he could beg for money from the church folks before they went into the church. (Because we all know what would have happened to the lame man if he had asked when they came out!) "Done put all that money in church; that preacher is always wanting money for this and that, auxiliaries selling tickets. I ain't giving that man nothing. I don't care if he is lame!" Now, if the church folks had known what it was, they would have taken the man in the church and fed him and taken care of him. That is what the church is supposed to do. The church has a responsibility to God to take care of His people. This man had been coming there for years begging money, and one day he encountered Peter and John going in the temple. He asked them for money and that's what he expected to get. But, Peter knew what it was, and he said, "Silver and gold have I none, but what I have I'll give you. In the name of Jesus Christ of Nazareth, rise up and walk." And when they touched him, immediately his feet and ankle bones received strength. And he jumped up and ran into the church, walking and leaping praising God. And the people looked in amazement. What is this?

Where does this power come from? After Jesus arose from the dead, He instructed His disciples for forty days. He instructed them not to leave Jerusalem until they had received the promise of the Father. He told them they would receive power after they received the Holy Ghost and should go into the world witnessing and preaching the word, First of all, we must all understand that the Holy Ghost is God! The third person in the Trinity. The Trinity is the three parts of the God head. The Father, Son, and the Holy Ghost. Jesus is the second person in the God head. As long as Jesus was here there was no need for the Holy Ghost. Jesus did everything for us. He fed us, He healed us, He instructed us, He raised us from the dead. So, when He left, we felt alone. We needed help. So, He said, "Let not your heart be troubled. Believe in God, believe in me also." And I will pray the Father and He shall give you another comforter that He will be with you forever. He will teach you all things and bring all things to your remembrance. The comforter is of the same quality and the same character as Christ. The comforter is God. Christ would go away, but the helper would remain forever. But, what is this? The first reference to the Holy Spirit was in Genesis, when the Earth had become dark and void and the Spirit of God moved upon the waters.

Further evidence was in Genesis, sixth day of creation, when God said, "Let us make man in our image and in our likeness." When Joshua led the Israelites across the Jordan, the Spirit of God parted the river and over forty thousand men passed over. It was the Spirit of God that gave Samson his great strength. The Spirit of God came over Saul in First Samuel, when he heard about the Amorites threatening the Jabesh people. David found out what it was when the Spirit of God came upon him before he fought Goliath. Solomon was instructed by God's Spirit when he asked for wisdom. Job was the first man recorded in the Bible to be told off by God's Holy Spirit. The Spirit of God actually had to leave the church in Ezekiel's day. The people were sinning so bad, he just got up and left. Ezekiel said the Spirit of the Lord was upon him and carried him up and put him down into a valley of dry bones.

As Jesus was growing up, He was constantly surrounded by angels ministering to Him and protecting Him. But, he did not heal anybody or cast out any devils until He received the Holy Spirit when He was being baptized by John the Baptist. It descended on Him in the form of a dove. Then, He received power and went out among the people preaching, teaching, and healing. No one could mess with that because He had on the full armor of God. Now, I know what they mean when the children of God sing, "Spirit of the living God, fall fresh on me." They know what it is! You cannot say you believe in God, but don't believe in the Holy Spirit. God is the Holy Spirit and the Holy Spirit is God.

We have to take the limits off of God. There is no impossibility when you're dealing with the God of the universe. He can be anything or do anything. The Bible said, "He is the Lily of the Valley, the Bright and Morning Star." The songwriter said:

We are often tossed and driven on the restless sea of time,
Somber skies and howling tempests often succeed a bright sunshine,
In that land of perfect day, when the mists have rolled away.
We will understand it better by and by.
By and by when the morning comes,
When the saints of God are gathered home.
We'll tell the story and we'll understand it better by and by.
We'll understand that God is Lord of lords, King of kings,
We'll know He is the Father, the Son, and Holy Spirit.
We'll believe that He created the world just by speaking the word.

You've Got What It Takes

2 Chronicles 32:6-7

And he set Captains of war over the people and gathered the people together to him in the gate of the city and spake comfortably to them saying, "Be strong and courageous, be not dismayed nor afraid, for the King of Assyria nor for all the multitudes that are with him. For there be more with us than with him." With him there is an arm of flesh, but with us, is the Lord our God to help us and to fight our battles. Or if you will, YOU'VE GOT WHAT IT TAKES!

Hezekiah, King of Judah, was a good king. He did all that was good in the sight of the Lord God. Ahaz, the King's father, had done all that was bad in the sight of the Lord. To give you a little background, he made idols for Balaam, burnt incense, even burnt his children in pagan sacrifices to the devil gods of Damascus. He burnt incense in all the high places and under every tree that was green. God finally got tired of him and delivered him and Judah into the hands of Israel and King of Syria. One day they lost 120,000 men in one day because they did evil in the sight of God. Did you ever see someone who seemed to get away with things that you wouldn't think about doing? Maybe they got away with it for months or maybe even years. Then, it seems all of the sudden nothing goes right for them. That was the situation Ahaz was in. As a result of sin, Judah was made slaves to their brothers Israel. Then, as always, God heard the cries of the people and sent the Prophet Obed to tell them to release their brothers and sisters, because their slavery was a result of wrath and judgement from God. So, they clothed them and fed them and sent them back to Jericho. But, Ahaz instead of being thankful, dug himself a deeper hole. God brought Judah low because of Ahaz' sins. Edomites, Philistines, and finally the King of Assyria came and attacked and carried away captives. Ahaz had paid

Assyria to help him, but they took his money and gave him more grief! But, Ahaz became worse and worse. He started sacrificing to their god's saying their gods help them. Ever hear that one? The grass always looks greener on the other side. But, God finally got tires of him and he died. Hezekiah became King when he was 25 years old and he restored everything that his father had destroyed. He reopened the temple and restored all that was destroyed. It took the Priests and Levites 16 days to cleanse the house of the Lord. Then, Hezekiah gathered all the rulers and people of the cities and made a covenant and sacrifice to God. They had a big revival. They brought in the choir and all the instruments and sang hymns. They got down on their knees and worshiped God from morning till late in the evening. Now days a preacher preaches more than 20 minutes and the church wants to fire him. The tithes and offerings were so immense that the priests had to build storage for them. The people then returned home and broke up all the false idols and gods and high places of sacrifice. Then, Hezekiah sent out a letter into all the tribes of Israel saying to return your hearts to the Lord God of Israel, the God of Abraham, Isaac, and Jacob. Hezekiah did all that was right in the sight of God and he and Judah prospered. So much that it was known in all the surrounding kingdoms. Then, like always, when you start living for God and let everyone know that you are a child of the King, trouble always comes. You might not have it right now, but trouble is on the way. And it seems like trouble always knows when to come. The King of Assyria came down and camped against the outer walls of Judah and threatened to destroy the city. Hezekiah had broken away from the deal his father had made with Assyria and the King threatened the Kingdom and Hezekiah apologized and offered to pay the King anything he wanted to leave him in peace. The price was so high that Hezekiah had to even strip the silver and gold off of the doors of the temple just to pay him, but the King of Assyria came to take the city anyway. He destroyed all the outlying tribes and was camped against Judah. The people became afraid because of the sheer numbers of the enemy. Some of the people wanted to ask

Egypt for help, but the Prophet Isaiah spoke against it. Then, the King of Assyria resorted to scare tactics because he knew he didn't have much time to take the city. Hezekiah had cut off the outside water supply and rerouted it under the wall and into the city. He sent messengers to talk against God and tell how they had conquered bigger cities than Judah, and their gods couldn't help them. Why should Judah be any different.

But, Judah had something the other tribes didn't have, something that allowed them to stand even in the face of unsurpassable odds. The situation worsened. Hezekiah and Isaiah had a little talk with God and He heard their prayers. Like in Psalm 40, "I waited patiently on the Lord, and He heard my cry." God told them not to worry because He had the situation well in hand. He promised them that not a single arrow would be fired in the city and that the King of Assyria would return home and be killed. That night, God sent an angel which killed 185,000 of the mighty men of Assyria and the Bible said they woke up the next morning corpses! Then the King of Assyria fled home in shame. He was later killed by his two sons while he was in the temple. The Lord delivered Hezekiah and all of Jerusalem. That's why in our everyday life, we've got to be of good courage, because for all good Christians, or children of God, there is trouble on the way. You don't have to worry, because one day you are going to wake up with a "giant," or trouble in your way. Once you become a child of God, there's always something that fights that inward person, so that when you want to do what's right, something is telling you to do wrong. There's something out there that makes trouble come when you least expect it. And trouble knows when to come at your weakest moment. Trouble will come when you're sick and down on your back, you're so sick that you cannot get up. Trouble will come when there's no friend around and you don't have anyone to talk to.

Trouble will come into your home when it isn't what it ought to be, and you're trying to treat your wife right and it seems that the better you get, the worse she gets. Trouble will come when you try to teach your family and your children right. It seems like the weight of the world gets on your shoulders. You can't get up and you fall to your knees and it seems like everything falls down on you. The mountain caved in on you last night and you get up and there's another mountain waiting for you. Early in the morning, there is a God somewhere. Paul and Hezekiah would say, "Don't give up. Hold to God's unchanging hand." There is a place made for you and me. You don't have to worry about it. Sin may be all around you. Trouble may be all around you, but I'm glad one day God said, "I'm coming back after my church without a spot or a wrinkle." I'm so glad He said, "I'll be with you even until the end of the world." I'm so glad that he said, "I go to prepare a place for you, so that where am, you may be also. In my Father's house there are many mansions. If it were not so, I would have told you." Come on up just a little bit higher. I've seen your work. I've trusted in you. You've done a good job. Come on up just a little bit higher. Pray your prayer. Sing your song. Do your thing, because God will make a way somehow. I haven't been what I am today all of my life. But, one day when was lying down on my bed of affliction, someone came into the hospital room, picked me up, cleaned me up, saved my soul, set me on fire, saying, "Go tell the world that the wages of sin is death. Tell them that I am the way, the truth, and the light. Go tell it on the mountain, go tell it in the valley. Preach the word in season and out of season, and I'll make a way somehow."

Don't Give Up Yet!

Are we all really happy to be here this morning?
Are we happy to praise his Holy Name?

Repeat after me. "I'm so glad to be in the house of the Lord this morning!"

Doesn't that feel good? Well, it ought to, because God didn't have to do it. Yet and still we come into his house wearing dead faces, singing dead songs, praying dead prayers, not encouraging the choir, not saying "Amen" to the preacher, and we expect God to bless us?

The word of God says to make a joyful noise unto the Lord, all ye lands. It also says to come before His presence with singing and praises. It also says to worship Him in spirit and in truth, which means that if you come to church and you just sit there and show no emotion whatsoever, and you do not get caught up in the spirit, then you're not being truthful either. Every day you wake up, God has blessed you, and that alone is cause for a celebration!

Joshua 7:1-12

We hear from the scriptures that Joshua had encountered a problem. And, it is no different from a lot of us. When we're going through our trials and tribulations, we feel as though God has left us. We feel that t-he problems of the world are too great and we give up on ourselves and we give up on God. God said that He will never leave us or forsake us. David said, "I've never seen the righteous forsaken or his seed out begging for bread. The problem is just like with a lot of us. We know how to get into trouble, but we don't know how to get out of it. II Chronicles 7:14 says that if my people who are called by my name shall humble themselves, and pray, and seek my face, and turn from their wicked ways, then shall I hear from Heaven and forgive their sins and heal their lands. Now Joshua knew this. That is why after he

41

fell at the battle between Israel and the men of Ai, He immediately tore his clothes and lay on his face and put dust on his head and began to seek the face of God. But, when God answered Joshua, he was like a lot of us. He wondered what would happen when the neighbors found out. God responded to Joshua by telling him, He did not want to hear his grief about all the men that were lost in the battle, but to get up and pursue the battle again!

God told Joshua that Israel had taken of the accursed thing and had put it even among their own things. God had commanded them to take only of the gold, silver, and vessels of brass and iron, for they were consecrated unto the Lord and were to be put in the Lord's house. Men, women, children, and all that they had had, must be destroyed because they were accursed unto God. As always, someone had disobeyed the word of God and all of Israel had to suffer because of it.

Now, we're all familiar with how God instructed Israel to march around Jericho for seven days and how the walls came tumbling down and God delivered the city into their hands. But, God told them up front that Jericho was accursed unto to Him, and that they not take anything out of the city except for what Got told them. They were also to burn the city. But just like now days, there is always someone that, no matter what God says, is going to do what he wants to anyway. The only people that were saved was the house of Rahab the Harlot. But Achan, one of Joshua's men, took of the accursed thing and dug a hole in the center of his tent and tried to hide it from God. It was already bad enough that he sinned, but he tried to cover it up. You can't hide sin from God. He had taken a Babylonian garment, two hundred shekels of silver, and fifty shekels of gold.

To this point, when Joshua was taking the land, God was with him. So, he sent out spies to spy out the land and they came back and said that Ai did not have many people. So only take two or three thousand men, that way the rest of the people could rest, and it should be no problem to take the city. Joshua agreed. When they went into the city, the men of Ai turned on them and ran them out, and killed thirty-six men, and Joshua's men became afraid. The Bible says their hearts melted and became as water. So, Joshua rent his clothes and went to God in prayer. (Makes no difference what the problem, I can go to God in prayer!) God told Joshua to get up and sanctify the people. He told him that as long as the unclean thing was among them, Israel could not stand before their enemies. God told him to bring all the people out, man by man, tribe by tribe, and God would tell him who did it. Then he and his entire household and all that he hath, along with the accursed thing, shall be burnt with fire, because he hath transgressed against God, and made a fool out of Israel before their enemies. After all the tribes were brought before him, Achan of the tribe of Judah was taken.

Joshua asked him to give God the glory and confess his sin. He said, "Well Joshua, first I saw it, it was pleasant to the eyes. Then I desired it, and I took it. Then I tried to hide it in the ground underneath my tent. Now, I'm sharing the penalty of my sin with all of my family." Joshua then dug up the accursed things and the Bible says he took Achan, his sons, his daughters, his oxen, his asses, and his wife, into a valley and burned them with fire. First, they were stoned. All sin affects others. There is no such thing as personal sin or private sin. The sin of Achan kindled the anger of God against Israel. The personal sin of believers always affects the church at large. Any time you sin, it affects all of us. After the sin was confessed and judgement carried out, God turned from his anger against Israel. Then God said to Joshua, "Do not be dismayed. Take all of the people of war with you, and arise, go up to Ai and take the land." So Joshua split the troops and had some lying in waiting behind the city and when morning came the people of Ai looked and saw Joshua camped out front. They then took every man in the city and went out against them. Then, God commanded Joshua to hold out his spear and the men in ambush attacked from the rear and burned the city with fire. (Watch your back) Then, when the men of Ai saw the fire, they tried to flee, but God delivered all twelve thousand of them into Joshua's hand. Then, they took the King and hanged him on a tree.

So, when trouble comes against you, don't give up. When it seems like you can't make it another day, don't give up. When you lose your job, don't give up yet. When you don't have enough money, don't give up yet.- When it seems you don't have enough religion, don't give up yet. If you're having problems with your family, or if you can't get along with your neighbors, or if you can't get along in your church, or if you are sick, or if it seems that everything in the world has come against you, don't give up. No matter what your problem is, whether it is cultural, theological, financial, racial, economical, physical, *NO MATTER WHAT IT IS, DON'T GIVE UP YET. GOD WILL DELIVER YOU!*

Don't Leave Until Your Work Is Done

A Bitter Taste Of Victory

John 20:28-30

After this, Jesus knowing that all things were now accomplished that the scripture might be fulfilled, saith, I thirst.

Now there was set a vessel full of vinegar, and they filled a sponge with vinegar, and put it upon hyssop, and put it to his mouth.

When Jesus, therefore had received the vinegar, he said, "It is finished." He bowed his head and gave up the ghost.

Sometimes in life, after being burdened down by things that we encounter in our every day routines in life, when given extra responsibility, we tend not to give our best. We take short cuts, push it aside, partially do, or we do nothing at all. Whether it is in our home, our job, our church, or with each other, we tend to be able to come up with every excuse in this world and the next, not to complete what we have started. Things that we enjoy doing we tend to perform effortlessly, and without regard to outside elements such as fatigue, prior commitments, work schedule, and all of those other things we're already doing up at that church. Things we do that cause us to warrant praise are sometimes honorable and are often time designed to show a certain talent or skill. They are easy to perform, because they are things that we like to do. But, the most important thing that you may be asked to do in your life, may also call for the biggest sacrifice. It will probably be something that you do not like to do, but because of the importance, it can not be left undone, and you are the only one available who can do it. It is important that certain things are not considered finished until they are completely done. Imagine a contractor building a house, but he leaves without putting the roof on. Imagine a pair of shoes without soles, a book without a cover, a car without an engine, or an elevator shaft without an elevator!

45

We would indeed notice immediately that something was missing or that someone had left before he had completed his job. Don't leave before your work is done. No one assigns you anything to do unless they first tell you what to do. They let you know, up front, what you must do to complete the task. Sometimes the hardest part is not the knowing, but the doing.

Christ also was faced with this problem. He stated that the Spirit of the Lord God was upon Him because He hath anointed me to preach the gospel to the poor. He hath sent me to heal the broken hearted, restore sight to the blind, and preach the acceptable year of the Lord. (Set at liberty they that are bruised.) Those were the easy things, but Christ also knew that He would be required to give His life for all of us! That was the hard part. Not many of us would give up our lives for our families, let alone a whole world full of people that you do not know and that had rejected you. Now, in order to complete any job, you must first start at the beginning. So, it was also with the job Christ had been given. He followed God's job specification to the letter, if you will.

1. First, Jesus sought out John the Baptist in the wilderness to be baptized by him. John felt unworthy to do this, but Jesus knew it had to be done for our example, so he told John to suffer it to be so. In other words, I can understand how you feel, but do it anyway. I have a job to do. John looked up and saw the Spirit of God descending on him like a dove. Then a voice from Heaven said, "This is my beloved son in whom I am well pleased."
2. Then, Jesus was led by the Spirit into the wilderness to be tempted by the Devil. The Devil waited until He had fasted 40 days and nights before he came to tempt Him. He caught Him while He was weak.
3. Then Jesus, walking by the sea, saw two brothers casting their nets into the sea. They were Peter and Andrew, his brother. He told them to follow Him and He would make them fisher's of men. Then, He called James and John and gathered the rest of the Twelve.

4. Then Jesus went all through Galilee, teaching in the Synagogues and preaching the gospel of the Kingdom. He healed all manner of sickness, cast out demons, and raised the dead.
5. He then went up and delivered the Sermon on the Mount.
6. Then, He taught them how to pray.
7. Then, He taught them saying, "Enter ye into the straight gate. For wide is the gate and broad is the way that leads to destruction. And many there be which go in thereat.
8. He healed Peter's mother-in-law. One of the disciples wanted to bury his father, and Jesus said, "Follow me, and let the dead bury their dead." Then He healed the Gadarene demonics. He gave sight to the blind.
9. Then, He gave His disciples power over unclean spirits and to heal all manner of sicknesses, and sent them out. Then, the fame of Jesus continued to spread abroad until the religious leaders became upset and started plotting His death. Peter shortly thereafter confessed that Jesus was the Christ. But, the Pharisees wanted a sign from Heaven.
10. Jesus went on and was transfigured in front of Peter, James, and John, his brother. He paid His taxes and moved on. Then He foretold His impending death to His disciples. He threw the money changers out of the temple after riding into town on a donkey, over palm branches and garments. He hungered and saw a fig tree and it had no fruit on it. So, Christ cursed the tree and it withered up and died.
11. Then, Jesus prepared the Last Supper before His death. Then, Jesus went off and prayed. Right there, in the garden of Gethsemane, is where the soldiers took Him. There, Christ performed His last miracle. Peter drew his sword and cut off the ear of a servant of the high priest. Jesus put it back on and healed him. Then, He was taken before Pilate to be tried in the middle of the night, about 3:00 A.M. Then Judas, who had betrayed Him, tried to get out of it by returning the 30 pieces of silver, but the priests refused it. Pilate's wife told him not to do it, but Pilate succumbed to the pressures.

Tell The Crucifixion Story

People said, "Give them Barabas." First they scourged Him, stripped Him, and put on Him a scarlet robe. Then, they took the robe off of Him and put His own clothes on Him. They then led Him the longest way to Calvary or Golgotha and crucified Him.

He was buried in a borrowed tomb. A rock sealed the entrance. Guards were posted. But on the third day, He got up, with all power in His hands. He's coming back again.

The Seven Last Words From The Cross

Matthew 27:46 "My God, My God, Why Has Thou Forsaken Me?" In verse 45 of the Gospel of Matthew it states, "Now, from the sixth hour there was darkness over all the land unto the ninth hour.

Matt. 27:46 ...and about the ninth hour, Jesus cried with a loud voice saying, "Eli, Eli, lama sabach' tha ni? Translated means, "My God, My God, why has thou forsaken me?"

From the sixth hour until the ninth hour, means from noon until 3:00 P.M. Mark indicates that Jesus had been placed on the cross at the third hour, which would be 9:00 A.M. The darkness was supernaturally imposed by God because there could be no other explanation. A full eclipse of the sun at full noon is an impossibility. God's wrath was poured out upon His Son during this period of darkness. What we have to understand is that Christ was in agony, because of the high price of atonement that he had to pay. He was accursed of God as our sin bearer. He suffered the agony of spiritual death for us. The sense of being forsaken was not necessarily caused by God the Father looking away from Him, but instead by looking at Him in wrath as He would a sinner in judgement.

God did not turn His back on the Son He loved, but on the sin that he hated. Psalm 22:1 David uttered these exact words that Christ uttered on the cross. Christ uttered these words loudly, because He was in pain. He was in pain bearing the price of a terrible impending death for the penalty of our sins, even though He was sinless. The Father loved Him because He had laid down His life for the sheep. The sorrow and suffering that Christ felt was unlike any we will ever experience, because He was an innocent man, sinless, but He was executed before God in our place. His heart was bitter. That is why when he yelled aloud, it made the earth quake and rent the rocks and graves opened up.

First, amidst all of this though, Christ, not once, doubted His Father's love for Him or His for His Father. But, His Father had forsaken him. He delivered Him up into the hands of His enemies and did not appear to deliver Him. Secondly, He let loose the powers of darkness against Him and suffered them to do their worst, worse than against Job. Third, no angel from Heaven was sent to deliver Him and no friend on Earth raised up to appear for Him. Fourth, He withdrew from Him the comfortable sense of God's presence with Him. When His soul was first troubled, He heard a voice from Heaven comforting him. In the garden, there appeared an angel from Heaven strengthening Him. But now, He had neither. God forsook Him. Not as He forsook Saul, but as He forsook David, leaving him despondent. Then, He let loose on His soul, a sense of wrath against man for his sin. Christ was made sin for us. Even though God loved Him as a Son, He frowned upon Him as a sinner for us.

Christ did not do as some of us would have in that same situation. He did not ask, "Why am I scourged?" Jesus could have asked questions such as why am I spit upon, or why was I nailed to the cross? He did not look down at His disciples and ask why have you forsaken me? He did not say why do you let my enemies banter me, ridicule me, place a crown of thorns on my head and make fun of me? He did not cry out and say to stop them from asking Him to come down from the cross. He did not ask why, people He had healed, would walk by Him and turn their backs on Him. But, when God turned His back on Him, Christ was concerned.

I Thirst

After this, Jesus, knowing that all things were now accomplished, that the scripture might be fulfilled, saith, "I thirst." Now, there was set a vessel full of vinegar (a strong wine) and they filled the sponge with vinegar, and put it upon hyssop and put it to his mouth. We know this to be true because John, witnessed the event and was close enough to Jesus to hear what He said. If we look at Matthew 27:47 it says that some who stood there said that this man called for Elias. Verse 48 says and straight way one of them ran and took a sponge and filled it with vinegar, put it on a reed and gave it to Him to drink. Now, if Christ had not said that I thirst, there would have been no reason for the man to have run for the wine with all of the other events that were taking place. Matthew just didn't hear Him and recorded what he heard and saw. John recorded the rest.

It was not strange that Christ was thirsty. In the beginning of Christ's journey for our redemption, He fasted for forty days and forty nights in the desert, while He was being tempted by the Devil. He was Hungry and He was thirsty. Christ was indeed thirsty again after all the toil, pain, suffering, and the hurrying that He had undergone, not to mention, the agonies of death. He was ready to expire purely from the loss of blood and the pain. But to make sure that the scriptures might be fulfilled, Christ was careful not to leave anything undone. Christ followed God's word completely. He did not do like some of us and leave out the bitter parts; He drank of the entire cup for us.

The torments of Hell were represented by the rich man that begged for a drop of water to cool his tongue. We would have been condemned to this type of Hell, if Christ had not intervened for us, if Christ had not suffered for us. Christ had endured all of the scourging and the crowning of Him with a crown of thorns, but He did not utter, oh my back, oh my head. He did not utter a single word. But, now he cried, "I Thirst." He was expressing His heart's desire. He thirsted after the glorifying of God and the accomplishment of His work of our redemption and the happy issue of His undertaking. Christ knew at this point that all else had been accomplished. He had to make sure that all scripture was fulfilled in Him. God was with Him. All that Christ did, even facing death, He did exactly according to the Word of God, taking care not to destroy, but to fulfill the words of the law and the prophets. First in Psalms, the scriptures had foretold His thirst. Now, He had to fulfill it.

Samson was a type of Christ. When he was laying the Philistines heaps upon heaps, he was sore a thirst. So, also, was Christ when He hung on the cross, spoiling principalities and

51

powers. Secondly, the scriptures foretold that in His thirst, He would be given vinegar to drink. He was given a drugged vinegar before He was crucified, but the prophecy was not fulfilled in that, because that was not in His thirst. Then, He would not drink, but now He took it. This should be proof to us that the words of God and the will of God is always done. Christ took the bitter with the sweet. In sin, we had forfeited all of the comforts and refreshments. We had in Eden, tasted the sour grapes. Therefore, they were also withheld, from Christ.

Heaven would not give Him any light. Earth would not give Him a drop of water, but Christ endured all of this for us. Where would we be now if Christ had not given His life for us? How would we be able to stand up against the powers of darkness to regain our rightful place in the presence of God? Christ not only gave his life for us, but in our place, He was beaten, He was mocked, He was taunted as HE hung upon the cross. He was put on public display, in front of His enemies, for a crime He did not commit. They had placed a crown of thorns on His head. He was separated from God and His soul tormented, bearing the burdens of our sins. But, through it all, Christ never turned back, until all was accomplished, and then He said, "I Thirst."

God Sent Me

Luke 4:14-21

And Jesus returned in the power of the Spirit into Galilee; and there went out a fame of Him, through all the region round about. And He taught in their synagogues, being glorified of all. And He came to Nazareth where He had been brought up, and as His custom was, He went up into the synagogue on the Sabbath Day and stood up for to read. And there was delivered unto Him, the book of the prophet Isaiah. And when He opened the book, He found the place where it was written. The Spirit of the Lord is upon me because He has anointed me to preach the gospel to the poor. He hath sent me to heal the broken hearted, to preach deliverance to the captives, and the recovering of sight to the blind, to set at liberty, them that are bruised. To preach the acceptable year of the Lord. And He closed the book and He gave it again unto the minister, and sat down. And the eyes of all of them that were in the Synagogue were fastened on Him. And He began to say unto them, "This day is this scripture fulfilled in your ears." God sent Me.

Everyone of us at one point or another in our lives was given a specific job to do. In being assigned that job, we are given a job description or a detailed outline of what our responsibilities are and what it will take to get the job done. Webster says a job is anything one has to do. A specific job is anything that is specially suited for a given use or purpose. Such was the case with Christ, when God sent His Son into the world. God knew what condition the world was in, so He prepared Christ for a specific job, and gave Him a detailed outline of all that He needed to get the job done.

After Jesus had fasted in the desert for forty days and forty nights, He continued in the power of the Spirit into Nazareth where He went to church, and read in the synagogue as was His custom. He read for all to hear what His earthly mission would entail.

Notes

I. TRINITY =
   A. The Lord God = Father
   B. The Lord God Christ = Son
   C. The Lord God Spirit = Holy Spirit

II. ANOINTED -
   A. Means to be set apart for a specific office or duty.
   1. Preach Gospel to Poor - First priority to give good things - good news - to the spiritually poor.
   2. Broken Hearted - Place bandages of healing on broken hearts - broken by sin and guilt.
   3. Deliverance to the Captives - People who were bound by Satan or a demon. Possessed would be free of their captors.
   4. Sight to the Blind - Open up the eyes of those who have been sinning so long, they have been spiritually blinded.
   5. Set at Liberty, them that are bruised - downtrodden shall be released from their oppressors - "LIFE." Bruised, you are not dead, or fatally wounded, but you're hurt. So, you're uncomfortable in your situation. You still hurt.
   6. Acceptable Year of the Lord - God is going to give blessings to all that come to Him - He has not come to judge yet, but to announce the coming Kingdom and to save sinners.

I Can See Clearly Now

John 9:24-25

Then again, they called the man that was blind, and said unto him, "Give God the praise; we know that this man is a sinner." He answered and said, "Whether he be a sinner, I know not; one thing know, that whereas I was blind, now I see." I can see clearly now. Many times, in all of our lives, we encounter many situations where we feel that we can't see something good enough or that our vision is being obscured for one reason or another. We try to move around or stand up or view whatever we're trying to look at from a different angle, in hopes that we can see it a little more clearly. Most of the time, no matter what angle you try to view it from, if there is enough blocking of your line of vision, or a large enough object, or obstacle in your way, it is very hard to see what you're looking at, clearly. Then, you realize that if you're going to ever see what you're trying to look at, you are going to have to move that object out of your way. Sometimes, you might even have to go up a little higher to look over that obstacle before you decide to remove it completely.

That is the way it is sometimes as we travel to and fro on our journey in a sinful world, full of every distraction possible, every materialistic mountain imaginable, anything and everything to block our vision, so that we can't see where our salvation is, or where our blessings come from. That is why every day of our lives, we are on the forefront of the battle line, and we have to put on the full armor of God so that we can move some of these things out of our way. For we wrestle, not against flesh or blood, but against principalities, against powers, the rulers of darkness of this world, against spiritual wickedness in high places.

Now Jesus, while He was in the world for a short period of time, He was constantly being challenged by everyone and everything that the Devil could put in his way. I am sorry to say that most of His problems were with church folks. They were constantly trying to say and do things to try and ruin His program, or get in the way of what He was trying to do. Much the same as it is today. Things haven't changed much in 2,000 years. But, we don't do that to our ministers today, do we? The scribes tried to put Christ in a dilemma. They brought Him first a woman who was caught in adultery during the Feast of Tabernacles. If He said the woman should be stoned, He would be violating Roman law. If He said she shouldn't, He would be violating Moses' law. They did this to try to entice sin, because they were spiritually blind. They could not see clearly. But Christ, after being pressed, wrote something on the ground then said, "He that is without sin, let him cast the first stone." Then, their conscience got the best of them and they walked out, one by one, leaving Christ and the woman. He told her to go and sin no more. He then began to preach and testify that He was the Light of the World. The deacon board (the Pharisees) objected. All testimonies had to be sustained by two witnesses. Christ said He knew where He came from, and where He was going, but they didn't, so they could disprove his testimony. He told them who their Father was, so they got mad and called Him "illegitimate." When He told them He existed before Abraham, they got mad and threw rocks at Him. But, He hid Himself and passed through the midst of them. As Jesus was passing by, He saw a man who was blind from birth. The disciples assumed that since he was blind, either he or his parents had sinned. But, Christ said neither had sinned, but the blindness gave an opportunity for God's power to be manifested. Then he spat on the ground and anointed his eyes and told him to go into the pool of Siloam.

The Bible says he went his way therefore and washed and came seeing. The neighbors saw him and said, "Isn't that he who was a blind beggar?" When Christ lifted the burdens of the world, an obstacle of being born in sin, out of his way, it even changed his appearance. When you get around, or away from sin, you even look different. Example: They got tired of arguing about it, and asked him, and he told them a man named Jesus opened my eyes. Then, the Pharisees asked him and he told them and they said Jesus was not of God, because He made clay on the Sabbath Day. Others said it was impossible for a sinner to perform miracles. They asked the man again, his opinion of Christ, and he said, "He is a prophet." They went and got his parents and asked them and they couldn't see the situation clearly and said it was their son and he was born blind, but how he received sight, they didn't know. They said, "Ask him, he's old enough." They didn't want the church folks to kick them out of the church. So, they called the man again and they asked him. He said, "I don't know if the man is a sinner, but one thing I do know is before I was blind, but now I see." Jesus lifted me, and my Bible tells me that those who wait upon the Lord shall renew their strength, they shall mount up with wings like eagles, they shall run and not be weary, and walk and not faint, because I waited patiently on the Lord and He healed me. He restored my sight and gave me a song to sing. He said I might have done a lot of wrong things in my life, but my change has come. I'm not the same as I used to be.

I can see clearly now. Can you?

Thanksgiving

I Samuel 6:9-19

Thanksgiving is defined in Webster as giving thanks or blessing. Tomorrow is a day set aside by our entire country to give thanks to God. It was originally instituted by the Pilgrims to give thanks to God for their survival. Thanksgiving is also defined as an expression of thanks, formal, often public, given to God in a form of prayer. A Pilgrim is a wanderer, or a traveler, in a foreign land.

So, we too are Pilgrims as we live our lives as Christians in the world we live in, but are not a part of. We live in a strange or foreign land. God has commanded us to come out from among them and be separate, and touch not the unclean thing. (II Cor. 6:17)

Exegesis of Psalm 100:

Make a joyful noise unto the Lord, all ye lands. Serve the Lord with gladness, come before his presence with singing. Means to give a glad shout and worship and praise unto God. All ye lands, refers to the entire Earth.

Notes

1. Ark had been in the house of Abinadab for over 70 years, then reign of Saul almost forgotten.
2. Transported on a new cart (was supposed to be on the shoulders of the priests).
3. No one could touch it or look in it - represented the presence of God. Uzziah touched it - God got angry - struck him down dead. (Oxen had shook it).
4. David became afraid - would not bring Ark into city of David. Took it to house of Obed-Edom for three months to allow God to cool off. Obed-Edom was blessed and this time David used more care in moving it.

Step By Step

II Chronicles 7:11-18

And the Lord appeared to Solomon by night, and said unto him, "I have heard thy prayer, and have chosen this place to myself for a house of sacrifice. If I shut up Heaven that there be no rain, or if I command the locusts to devour the land, or if I send a pestilence among my people; (contagious disease) if my people, who are called by my name, shall humble themselves and pray, and seek my face, and turn from their wicked ways, then will I hear from Heaven, and will forgive their sin and heal their land. Now, mine eyes shall be open and mine ears attend unto the prayer that is made in this place. For now have I chosen and sanctified this house, that my name may be there forever, and my eyes and my heart shall be there perpetually (lasting or enduring forever). And as for thee, if thou wilt walk before me, as David thy Father walked, and do according to all that I have commanded thee, and shalt observe my statutes and my judgments. Then, will I establish the throne of thy Kingdom, according as I have covenanted with David, thy father saying, there shalt not fail thee a man to be ruler in Israel."

God's Four Steps to Victory

When we think of steps, we think of steps in a number of ways. Sometimes in life, we take a step. Sometimes, we walk a few steps. We sometimes take a step forward and often times, we take a step backwards. We walk up steps, and we also walk down steps. Sometimes, we get up or down the steps and we find that the door at the top or the bottom of the stairs is closed: Meaning that we can go no further up the steps or down. Sometimes we get so high up the steps that we forget that we started at the bottom to get to the top, and the same steps that we came up, we will have to go back down. (Be careful what you do on your way up the steps!) Some of the same folks you pass going up the steps, you will see on the way back down! Sometimes, we can step so far down that down seems like up!

In life, we are sometimes in step, and other times we are out of step. We step in, and sometimes we are steppin' out! Sometimes, we even break step. Sometimes, we keep step, sometimes, we're out of step. Sometimes, we step on it and sometimes, it steps on us; or sometimes, we take it step by step. (Gradually in degrees.) In "Webster's," it says if you take steps, it means to adopt certain means or measures; or to provide steps specifically. God has provided us with steps; steps to take; a certain means or measure, provided specifically, that you may receive your blessing and go on to victory. If we look at our text, we see that God is addressing Solomon, the King. David's son, to whom it was predestined by the direct will of God, that he be the one to build the Temple of the Lord. Even though it was in David's heart to build a house for the Lord, God said the fact that it was in his heart was good enough.

But, it would be Solomon who would build it. In Psalm 132:4, David states that he will not settle comfortably into his own home until he had established a permanent resting place for the Ark of God. This is a great contrast to a lot of us today who sit up in our big houses with plenty to eat and too much furniture, while our brothers and sisters are starving, living in the streets with no roof over their heads, while we go to great lengths to make ourselves more comfortable. David did not do that. His service was first to God, then to himself. As a result of David's righteousness and faithfulness, he prospered, and so did his descendants. For I have never seen the righteous forsaken or his seed out begging bread.

This is an example we all should follow. Not only will we be blessed, but the seed or our families, also. We change,, but God is immutable. He's the same today as He was yesterday, as He will be forever. Solomon's worship at Jerusalem was impossible, apart from a completed temple. He had no place to worship God in Spirit and in truth. Imagine coming here next

Sunday and there is no church here. We might have service, but we'd know something was missing. It took Solomon 20 years to complete the building of the Lord's house and his own. It took 7 years to build the temple and 13 for his own house. Prior to where we pick up our text, Solomon had completed the temple. He intentionally waited many months, that it might coincide with the great Harvest Feast of Tabernacles. All of Israel was gathered together on this occasion to give sacrifice to God. The first thing that Solomon did was to appoint priests from the tribe of Levi to bear the Ark into the Holy of Holies in the temple. All the priests and Levites then began singing and praising God and blowing trumpets singing, *"For He is good and His mercy endureth forever."* Then, the Glory of God appeared in the form of a cloud so thick that the priests could not minister and had to leave. By God entering in a cloud, He gave His acceptance the same way as He did the Tabernacle of Moses in Exodus 40:34.

All the priests had to leave in order for the rightful owner to come in. In order for God to come into our hearts, we have to make room. Also note, it was when they were singing and playing all in one accord that the Glory of God entered the temple. Solomon had built the house for the glory and honor of God, and God gave His approval. When Solomon saw the presence of the Lord, He gave a testimony and a prayer before all the people and God sent down fire from Heaven that consumed the entire altar and the Glory of God filled the house. Then, the Lord appeared to Solomon by night and outlined His steps for a national blessing.

1. God promised to own this house for a house of sacrifice to Israel and a house of prayer for all people.
2. He promised to answer the prayers of all the people. ("There will I make myself known, and there will I be called upon.")
3. National judgments are discussed. Famine, pestilence, and perhaps war. For by locusts devouring the land may be meant enemies as greedy as locusts and laying the entire land to waste. Unity of prayer, repentance, and reformation

are required. God expects His people that are called by His name, if they dishonor it, should honor it, by accepting the punishment of their iniquity. (Wickedness or sin.)

4. They must humble themselves under His hand, and pray for the removal of the judgement. And yet, all this will not do unless they turn from their wicked ways, and return to God.

5. God will forgive their sin, which brought the judgement upon them, and then heal their land and redress all of their grievances.

God Will Be There With You!

Daniel 3:23-25

23: And these three men, Shadrach, Meshach, and Abednego, fell down bound into the midst of the burning fiery furnace. 24: Then Nebuchadnezzar the King, was astonished, and rose up in haste, and spake, and said unto his counselors, "Did not we cast three men bound into the midst of the fire?" They answered and said unto the King, "True, Oh King." 25: He answered and said, "Lo, I see four men loose, walking in the midst of the fire, and they have no hurt; and the form of the fourth is like the Son of God."

God will be there with you!

Sometimes in our lives, as we go through our trials, tribulations, and worldly situations, we sometimes feel as though we are going through these things by ourselves. We feel as though maybe God has forgotten about us, or God doesn't care about our particular situation. Maybe, we feel that we are not important enough to warrant God's attention, or maybe that God doesn't get involved anymore. So, we tend to tolerate, and to put up with, a lot of situations simply because we feel that there is no solution. But, I came here to confirm to you this day, that no matter who you are, or where you came from, no matter how much money you have, or what your position is in life; no matter what your problem is, whether it's cultural, physical, financial, psychological, or theological; no matter what it is you're going through, God will not only help you but, GOD WILL BE THERE WITH YOU!

In the beginning, when God created the heavens and the Earth, God formed the birds in the air, the beasts of the fields, the fish and whales in the sea. He reformed the Earth, and formed man, and placed him in the garden to have dominion over all that He had created. But, God did not just place Adam in the garden, He spent time with Him; He instructed him. I remember David saying in Psalm 139:7-10, "Whither shall I go from thy spirit? Or whither shall I flee from thy presence? If I ascend into Heaven, thou art there. If I make my bed in Hell, thou art there. If I take the wings of the morning and dwell in the uttermost parts of the sea, behold thou art there. Even there shall thy hand lead me, and thy right hand shall hold me." Where can I go? God is everywhere.

When the children of Israel traveled through their 40 years in the desert, God led them as a cloud by day and a pillar of fire by night. God wanted them to know that no matter what they came up against, that not only would He make a way out of no way, but God would be right there with them. When Moses went before Pharaoh, God was there with him.

Likewise, when King Nebuchadnezzar made a golden image over 90 feet tall and sent out a decree that everyone in the Kingdom, at an appointed time, should bow down and worship the idol. He sent this decree into all of his Kingdom. To all the princes, rulers, governors, and to anyone who had a position in his kingdom. He said that whenever the instruments played that everyone in the Kingdom was to bow down and worship the idol. Anyone who did not, in the same hour, would be cast into the middle of a burning fiery furnace. Therefore, at the time when all the people heard the sound of the instruments, the Chaldeans, who were very envious of the position of the Jewish men Shadrach, Meshach, and Abednego came near and watched them. When they did not bow down and worship the idol, they went and told King Nebuchadnezzar. They told the King that these men whom he set over his affairs in Babylon, did not worship his gods nor the golden image that he had set up. Then the King became furious and sent for the three men. He then questioned them as to their actions and gave them another chance to obey. They refused. Their reply was that their God, whom they served was able to deliver them from the fiery furnace, but whether He did or not was up to His will. They would faithfully serve Him regardless. So, in any event, they would be delivered either by life or death. The King became angrier and commanded that the furnace be made seven times hotter and commanded the most mighty men in his army to bind them up and cast them into the furnace.

The flame was so hot that it slew the men that cast them into it. The three men fell into the center of the furnace. Then, the King looked through the side of the furnace and was shocked and surprised to see them in the midst of the furnace unharmed. They were not alone. He inquired of his counselors, "Did we not cast three men, bound, into the furnace?" They answered and said, "True, but I see four men loose, walking about, and one looks like the Son of God. The King then called them to come out, and not a hair of their heads nor their clothing was singed. Then, the King said, "Blessed be the God of Shadrach, Meshach and Abednego. And if anyone should say anything amiss about Him, that he shall be cut into pieces and their houses shall be made a dunghill." No other God can deliver after this sort.

God was there for Shadrach, Meshach, and Abednego. He will be there for you.

Hear Our Prayer, Oh Lord

Matthew 6:7-13 Lord's Prayer

"But, when you pray, use not vain repetitions as the heathen do. For they think that they shall be heard for their much speaking. Be not ye, therefore, like unto them. For your Father knoweth what things ye have need of, before you ask Him. After this manner, therefore, pray ye:

"Our Father, who art in heaven, hallowed be thy name. Thy Kingdom come. Thy will be done, in Earth as it is in Heaven. Give us this day our daily bread. And forgive us our debts as we forgive our debtors. And lead us not into temptation, but deliver us from evil. For thine is the Kingdom, and the power, and the glory, forever, Amen."

Prayer:

Have any of us had a talk with God, lately? Have we been sufficiently blessed and uplifted by the many things He has bestowed upon us? In other words, has God done anything for you lately? If He has, the Word says that the redeemed of the Lord ought to say so! God is good to all of us. He causes the sun to shine every day. He causes the flowers and the grass and the trees to come up in all their majesty and their beauty. He causes the rain to fall upon the Earth; the seasons to change; the snow to fall. He gives us air to breathe to sustain us; water to drink, so we're not thirsty. He gives us a reasonable portion of health and strength. God has been good to us.

Do any of you believe that God answers prayer? If I didn't believe that God answers prayer, I'd quit praying. Webster's Dictionary says that prayer is any spiritual communion with God. A request or a petition. All of the great men and women in the Bible prayed constantly. David said, "I waited patiently on the Lord and He inclined unto me and He heard my cry. He reached down into a horrible pit into the miry clay, set my feet upon a rock, and established my going. He put a new song in my mouth." God not only listened to David, but, He inclined unto him and answered him! David had sinned and he prayed to God, and God answered him. All of us were born in sin. All of us have lived low down dirty lives. All of us need to be cleansed. Have you ever seen folks in desperate need of prayer? Have you seen a junkie? Have you ever seen an alcoholic? Have you ever seen a prostitute, a street walker, little girls 15 and 16, walking the streets, hustling money, looking like they're 90!

Let me tell you something. It doesn't matter who you are or where you come from or if you're 16 looking 90. You can pray to God and He'll answer you. It's good to know that even if you're a nobody from nowhere, that you can ring up the Lord of lords, King of kings, and that He'll incline unto you and He'll listen to you. You sometimes, here, can't even get a friend to listen to you, but you can ring up God and He'll listen to you! There are times in your life when you need to be put up, shut up, set up, cleaned up, and you should always be prayed up!

After Christ was tempted in the wilderness by Satan and started His ministry through all of Galilee, He encountered a large multitude of people who had been following Him from all the places around Galilee where He had preached. So, He retreated into the mountains so that He could spend some time with His disciples, and so He could teach them. He told them not to pray as the heathen do. Do not make vain repetitions. In other words, we are not supposed to pray the same type of prayer as the non-believer, and we are not to try to wear God by repeating it over and over again! It is not the length of the prayer, but the strength of the prayer! Be ye not therefore like unto them. For your Father knows what things ye have need of, before you ask. God, through His foreknowledge, knows everything. Someone says then why should we pray? You should pray because by praying to God, you are acknowledging the fact that you realize that no matter what the situation is, that you have faith that God will work it out for you somehow.

By saying, "Our Father, which art in Heaven, hallowed be thy name," you are showing that you accept the fact that God is your Father and that you are in awe of His holiness, and that you hold Him in reverence. Only a child of God who has been born again, can rightly claim God as his Father and pray this prayer with confidence, expecting an answer.

"Thy Kingdom come, thy will be done on Earth as it is in Heaven." It means that we should always pray for the Kingdom of God and it's effective reign upon the Earth. That also, our will shall conform to the will of God, just as it is in Heaven. Many of us want to do what we want to do. God's will, through His decrees, predestination, direct will, and foreknowledge, will be done.

Give us this day our daily bread, means not only our provision of food in general, but also our spiritual nourishment. It does not profit you to be physically full, but spiritually starving. (Manna, etc.)

And forgive us our debts as we forgive our debtors. It means that we should ask God to forgive us for our sins which are our moral and spiritual debts to God. We are also to forgive those who have committed an offense against us.

And lead us not into temptation, but deliver us from evil, means that we are asking God to help us in our daily confrontations with the sins and spiritual wickedness of this world. We are not saying that God leads us into doing evil, but through His permissive will, He allows certain things to happen to test our commitment to Him. (Job)

For thine is the Kingdom, and the power, and the glory, forever, AMEN, means that we are praising God and acknowledging that everything is God's. We are God's. He has all power and glory through all eternity.

Hear our prayer, oh Lord.

Giving God The Praise In The Midst Of A Bad Situation

Psalm 22:22-31

I will declare thy name unto the brethren, in the midst of the congregation, I will praise thee. Ye that fear the Lord, praise Him. All ye seed of Jacob, glorify Him. Fear Him all ye the seed of Israel, for He hath not despised nor abhorred the affliction of the afflicted. Neither has He hid His face from them, but when he cried unto Him, He heard. My praise shall be of thee in the great congregation. I will pay my vows before them that fear Him. The meek shall eat and be satisfied; they shall praise the Lord, that seek Him; your heart shall live forever. All the ends of the world shall remember and turn unto the Lord, and all the kindred of the nations shall worship before thee. For the Kingdom is the Lord's, and He is governor among the nations.

God has been mighty good to all of us. In the midst of every situation, no matter how difficult we had perceived it to be. God had been right there with us. Through victory, or in times of trouble, God has never forsaken us. The Bible says, that David said, "I have never seen the righteous forsaken or their seed out begging for bread." David lived a long time and a long time ago.

It is easy to give God the praise when things are going right. When we get that new car, or that raise on our job, or we get that coat or that dress that we wanted, or new china in the closet. We get all worked up and we want to praise the Lord. But yet and still, we come into the house of the Lord and we sit there like we don't know that the Lord has been good to us, and that God has brought us a mighty long way. The book says if God has been good to you, the redeemer in you ought to say so. Somebody ought to praise the Lord!

David, the King, had been through many trials and tribulations in his life, but God had also granted him many victories.

73

David was King over all of Israel. He was in a position of responsibility, to the people and to God. David was chosen of all the men in the land because God said that He wanted a man after His own heart. But, David fell when he lay with Bathsheeba. He sinned and he had to pay a price. God spared his life, because of his repentance, but David had to pay a terrible price. Their was turmoil in his Kingdom almost to the day he died. All of Israel had to suffer for David's sin. When David wrote this Psalm, he was in danger, fleeing for his life. But, the bad part was, he was fleeing from his son, Absolom. Nathan, the prophet, told David that there would be days like this. The problem started when David's son, Ammon, lusted after his daughter, Tamar, who was also David's son, Absolom's sister. He loved her so much that he made himself sick and asked the King if he would send Tamar to his home to dress him some meat. She was ready to prepare it, but Ammon refused to eat. He then sent out all of the men and made advances toward her. She tried to tell him it was evil, but he forced her anyway. Then, he got mad and kicked her out.

There is a thin line between love and hate. Now Tamar was wearing a robe of many colors. This told all the Kingdom that she was one of the King's daughters that was still a virgin. She tried to tell Ammon that he was only making it worse by kicking her out, because now, not only had he slept with her, but he kicked her out and abandoned her. She would be disgraced. Ammon did not care. He told his men to kick her out and bolt the door behind her, also. Broken hearted, she went and told her brother Absolom. He plotted for two years and had his brother killed at a feast after he got drunk. He then fled the Kingdom and stayed in a city on his mother's side!

David, after a couple of years, allowed him back, but would not see him. Meanwhile, for four years, Absolom plotted to overthrow the Kingdom. Absolom was a politician. He saddled up his chariot and had fifty men run before him and stood in the King's gates and talked to everyone who went into the King for judgment. He found out where they were from, and then offered sympathy for their situation. He said that if he were David, he would rule in their favor, but since he did not have that authority, he could not help them. He won the hearts of the people and four years later ran David out of Jerusalem. So, David and his closest friends, the Gittites fled. Finally, David mustered up enough support to go against Absolom and Israel. He killed more than twenty thousand men that day. Absolom, in the middle of the battle, was fighting against the men of David sitting upon a mule, and rode into a tree and hanged himself. The Lord had avenged David. A servant had to bring David the news. He sat on the castle wall and mourned. So, instead of a day of celebrating the victory, it was a day of mourning, because of David's personal loss.

The Lord, by avenging David, gave David the victory. God also gave David a reason to praise him, even in a bad situation.

Our Time Has Come

Matthew 3:1-3

In those days came John the Baptist, preaching in the wilderness of Judea. And saying, "Repent, for the Kingdom of Heaven of Heaven is at hand." For this is he that was spoken of by the prophet, Esaias (Isaiah) saying, "The voice of one crying in the wilderness, prepare ye the way of the Lord, make His path straight.

Our Time Has Come!

In today's society, we live in a very now world. By this mean, we want everything instantly. When we put the key in the ignition, we want the car to start right up. When we pull or push the button, we want the television set to come right on, with sound. We don't have time to perk coffee, so we use instant. We have instant food, microwaves, and take out service at our restaurants. We want everything now.

Some things need preparation. Preparation, so that we can appreciate the significance or the goodness. Before you turned the key in that ignition, someone spent a lot of time building and preparing that car so that you could do that. Before we pushed the button on that television, someone else built that television set, so that when you pulled the button, you would have a picture and sound. Somebody picked those coffee beans and those tea leaves so that you could have instant coffee or tea. Time and preparation are important. I heard a man on television say that we will sell no wine before it's time. But, somebody smashed the grapes and aged them and bottled them ' and labeled them and sold them. The proper preparation was made so that when the man came into your living room on the television set saying, "We will sell no wine before it's time," he had something to give you.

Our Time Has Come.

77

Preparation is important. Many times if things are not properly prepared for you it is rejected, because you don't understand the significance or importance of the situation. Politicians campaign for years before the elections preparing you so that you don't forget that the election is coming, and to let you know what you can expect when their man takes office. Preachers preach at a church, sometimes many times before a church will call them to Pastor, so that the church can be prepared for the type of a man they will be getting. Preparation is important.

The period in the Bible between Malachi and Matthew are often referred to as the silent years. For that period of about 400 years before the birth of Christ, God had been silent. No one had heard from God in 400 years. He had sent no prophet or deliverer for His people. But, the events of this period made way for the birth and the ministry of John the Baptist, and the ministry of Christ.

Under the Persians, the office of High Priest, was transformed to a political office with great power. Murders were committed because people wanted to be High Priest. Alexander the Great defeated the Persians and dealt kindly with the Jews. The Egyptians ruled. Then, the Syrians ruled. They forced the Jews to eat swine, which they were prohibited to do by God. They also erected an altar to Jupiter on the old altar of burnt offerings. Copies of the scriptures were burned. The oppressed were not long in finding a champion. When the Syrians made a visit expecting the old High Priest, Matthias, to offer the pagan sacrifice, he killed an apostate Jew at the altar, along with the Syrian officer who was presiding and started a revolution. He fled to the Judean Highlands and waged guerrilla warfare against them. He did not live to see his country freed, but he commissioned his sons to carry it out. Judas, nicknamed the Maccabee, took control after his father's death. That's where we get the group of people referred to as the Maccabees. Then Pompey, defeated the Maccabees, and took over from Rome during a period of civil war among the people. It was here that your Scribes, Sadducees, and Pharisees became powerful. Herod, then with Roman support, became King of the Jews. He was the most cruel ruler of his time. He was the one who had all the babies slain at the birth of Christ in Bethlehem. Jews became divided. Some stuck to the old religion of their fathers, while others went with the Hellenists, or the new religion. Hellenists were simply Jews who adopted the Greek language, and along with it, lifestyles and practices. We have that same situation today, but the Bible foretold that people would listen to this new Gospel with itching ears, and reject the real True Gospel.

To have religion is dangerous. To have religion and not Jesus Christ is eternal damnation. You have to repent of your sins and except Christ as your personal Savior. There was such division and confusion that it necessitated the need for John the Baptist's message of repentance and baptism. John was the forerunner of Christ. He was the son of Zacharias and Elizabeth, and the cousin of Jesus. The significance of this preparatory ministry can not be estimated. John's birth was announced by the angel, Gabriel. John's father was a priest. His birth was accompanied by a promise, "He shall be great in the sight of the Lord and filled with the Holy Ghost." Jesus said that none was greater than John the Baptist.

John means in Hebrew, "God is gracious," because you see we were about to enter a period of grace. Through grace, God allowed John to prepare the people and make the way straight for the Lord.

Tell the story of John the Baptist.

John was not like our preacher of today with shiny shoes, Pierre Cardin suits, and wavy hair. John wore only clothing made from camel's hair, a leather girdle, and homemade sandals, not Giorgi Brutini. He did not eat at fancy restaurants. He ate locusts and wild honey. But, he preached the Gospel in season and out of season, all through Judea. He preached the entire area around the Jordan and many came to him to be baptized and repent. For you see water and no repentance is not good. John's ministry was well received in it's early stages. Even the Scribes and the Pharisees came to hear him. But, John challenged the system. He asked for proof of what the Pharisees were teaching. This made them mad because there was none. What they were teaching was unscriptural! They believed that Abraham, being their ancestor, guaranteed their salvation. But not so. John told them God could use the rocks and raise children to Abraham. Repentance is a personal thing. It is an inward and outward change; a new way of life without sin. He also said, a tree that does not produce good fruit is chopped down. You better check out what type of fruit you're bearing, so that you don't get chopped down. Our Time Has Come. Our time has come to take a good look at ourselves to determine what our position is in Christ. Our time has come for a new beginning!

God's Message For The Last Days

John 3:16-17 For God so loved the world that He gave His only begotten Son, so that whosoever believeth in Him should not perish, but have everlasting life. For God sent not His Son into the world to condemn the world. (Amos 5:18-20)

Since the beginning of our existence, God has been speaking to us. When God created Adam, He spoke to him face to face in the Garden of Eden. He walked and talked with him, counseled him, fed him, took care of him. He gave him responsibility. He gave him dominion over the fish and the great whales of the sea. Man was God's son, made in His image. God looked upon him and said that it was good. When he began to feel alone, God put him in a deep sleep, and took a rib from the part closest to his heart, and formed woman. Then, He awoke Adam from his sleep and presented her to him, and Adam looked and saw woman in all of her beauty and said that it was real good! Not getting off track, but I want to touch on a little of this, because I feel that a misunderstanding of this portion of scripture is what caused a lot of our problems and heartaches. You see, after God put Adam to sleep and fashioned Eve and brought her to the man, Eve was a grown woman. The first thing she saw was God. She placed her hand in God's hand. After she showed faith and trust in God by letting God guide her, God took her to Adam! I have a little advice for some of you woman. Seek God first, then let Him find Adam. God knows where Adam is. Even then, God was giving man a message, for you see Adam still had a problem. Adam was 1/2 man and Eve was 1/2 woman. You put the two together and you have a whole. Adam's side was missing. Eve had it. Adam wanted it, so there was your first marriage ceremony. They became one. God put man in a needy situation. He showed man he was only half the man he thought he was. Woman was created to bring out the deficiencies in man and to make up the deficit for what man was lacking. Needless to say, this situation did not last for long. Man fell out of grace with God. Sin entered the world because man was disobedient. Man was in a terrible position. No matter how he tried to renew that fellowship with God, he fell short. The situation became worse. Man was trying to restore himself, but was unsuccessful. As a matter of fact, man became so sinful that God flooded the entire world just to get man out of His sight. But thank God, Noah was faithful, and God spared Noah and his family. Noah had a son named Shem, who fathered a son named Abram, who later became Abraham. It was through Abraham that God's promise to the world was fulfilled. You see, God knew that man needed help. Man needed a Savior. God sent Abraham, Isaac, and Jacob. He sent Joseph over Egypt. He sent Moses as His instrument in Egypt. He gave him Aaron as a helper. He gave Moses the Law.

After the era of Moses, God sent Joshua to continue the conquest. Then, God sent judges and kings. David and Solomon rebuilt the temple that God was to live in. Then, He sent prophets from Isaiah to Malachi, Daniel, Jeremiah, and Ezekiel. A whole host of them, but none of them could redeem man to his rightful position with God. It's not by might; it's not by power, it's through my spirit. You can't do it, the preacher can't do it, your wife can't do it, etc. God, has to do it! God commanded His love toward us, in that while we were yet sinners, Christ died for us. Our time has come.

Easter

(The Way It Should Be)

Even though "Easter Bunnies" and "Jelly Beans" are good and provide us with some type of festive spirit, they sometimes hide the real meaning of Easter. We sometimes get so caught up in all the things created by retailers and merchandisers to get you into their place of business, that we forget about all of the things that our heavenly Father has done to get us into His place of business. Now, I've got a problem with that, because the real reason for Easter is to have an opportunity to proclaim to the world that Christ gave up His life, and rose again, so that we could be redeemed back to God.

Cor. 5:15 in the Living Bible states, "He died for all so that all who live, having received eternal life from Him, might live no longer for themselves, live their lives to please themselves, but to spend their lives pleasing Christ. Yes, men give us Easter Bunnies and Jelly Beans, but Christ gave His life, so that we could have life, and have it more abundantly. Easter is celebrated in many ways. The word Easter in used only once in the King James version.

(Acts 12:4) It is a mistranslation. The proper translation is Passover. It was originally a Spring Festival in honor of Eastra or Ostara, a teutonic goddess. This name was transferred to the paschal feast sometimes after the close of the New Testament. It is very important for us to realize that there is nothing wrong with dressing up and taking part in all of the other things associated with Easter as long as we understand the real meaning of Easter, and put Christ first in all that you do. The Hebrews, by sacrificing the first fruits of their barley harvest, gave significance to Christ's resurrection. All people die because they are related to Adam. Being members of a sinful race, and where there is sin, death results. All who are related to Christ will one day rise again.

God bless you all in this holiday season.
Put Christ first this Easter Sunday.

You Are Just What God Is Looking For!

Timothy 3:13   Acts 1:16-17   Acts 6:1-8

The success of any officer must always depend, mainly upon his qualifications, to perform the duties of the office. Incompetent men or women in the deaconship or the ministry prove to be a burden upon the cause the appointment was intended to promote.

As it is told in the book of Acts, the first deacons were called because of a rift between the Grecians and Hebrews. Both of these groups were Jewish. The problem came down to money. The Grecians were Greek speaking Jews and the Hebrews were the traditional, Aramaic speaking Jews. The problem was that most of the wealthy Christians had sold all of their goods to provide for the poor. Now, some of the Grecian Jews felt that some of their poor and widows were being neglected in favor of some of the traditional Aramaic speaking Jews. Does that sound familiar? People put their money in church because they say that they want to be obedient to the covenant and the word of God. Then, they murmur about how it's being used! We are to contribute cheerfully and regularly, as God has prospered us.

So, the twelve disciples called all of the disciples together and reasoned that it was not good for them to have to devote their time and leave the word of God to wait tables. Thus, the twelve decided to look among the congregation and to seek out seven men of good reputation, filled with the Holy Spirit. Men, who could be responsible for administering the charitable contributions, and work among the people. This would allow the apostles to concentrate on their main responsibility of the ministry they were called to, which was prayer, preaching, and teaching the word of God. We would do well today to follow that example. Some pastors today do not have the time to devote themselves fully to prayer and the word of God, because they are getting all tied up in every little thing and problem in the congregation. The deacons have a responsibility to free up the pastor to do the job to which he has been called. They agreed to do this, and chose seven men. They were brought before the apostles who prayed and laid hands on them. The scripture then goes on to say that the word of God increased, disciples multiplied, and a great company of priests were obedient to the faith. Then, the scripture singles out Stephen, because he was full of faith and power. He was what God was looking for. One day we looked out among ourselves and chose Brother Paul Hayes, because we knew that he was just what God was looking for. Bold and full of faith.

What Is God Looking For In A Deacon?

In First Timothy 31-10, the scripture says that there are seven qualifications that God is looking for in a deacon.

1. Grave not double tongued.
2. Not given to much wine.
3. Not greedy of filthy lucre.
4. The faith.
5. Proved.
6. Pure conscience.
7. Husbands of one wife.

Now, when God says He is looking for a deacon that is grave, not double tongued, He doesn't mean dead and quiet. He means He is looking for a man who is serious and doesn't say one thing and do another. In the Bible, scripture continually advises against strong drink. In today's society, putting all things relative, it means "No Drinking!" Not greedy of filthy lucre; the temptation is there, even for the most Godly deacon. But, it cannot be tolerated, because the love of money is the root of all evil. The faith to be a deacon; a man must be grounded in the faith, because belief is the basis for behavior. Let the deacons be husbands of one wife, ruling their children and their houses, well. Now, being husbands of one wife does not mean that a deacon cannot be a man that has been divorced or single. In the Bible days, it was a practice to have more than one wife. Some kings had hundreds. God was not looking for this. He wanted His ministers and deacons to have one wife, not one at home and one across town. It goes on to say, ruling their children, well, and their own houses. In other words, if you do not have control over your own house, and you can't keep your children in order, how are you going to deal with God's children? For we have used the office of deacon well purchase to themselves a good degree, and great boldness in the faith which is Christ Jesus. It means that being a deacon gives you respect in the church. You live in a glass house. You have to have confidence and assurance to speak with authority.

This is just what God is looking for!

God Is On Your Side!

Let them now that fear the Lord say, That His mercy endureth forever. I called upon the Lord when I was in distress and the Lord answered me and set me in a large place. The Lord is on my side, what can man do unto me? The Lord taketh my part with them that help me. It is better to trust in the Lord than to put confidence in man.

Romans 8:31 states that if God be for you who can be against you?

Like many of you, I was brought up in a religion that I believe had some error in it. We were taught that God was unreachable. He was sitting somewhere way up there with a long white beard and flashing red eyes waiting for us to do something wrong or to step out of line so that He could smash us and bring immediate judgement. As soon as we would step out of line, God would look down and smash us with that rod of iron. It was like God was way up there and we were way down here and God was somehow against us! We know that the Bible states that if we try to hide, no matter where we go even in Hell, God will find us! God was constantly checking up on us waiting for us to make a mistake so that He could clobber us.

That Is Not The God Of The Book.

John 3:16 states that God so loved the world that He gave His only begotten Son, so that whosoever, (we are that whosoever), believeth in Him should not perish, but have everlasting life. God sent not His Son into the world to condemn the world, but that the world through him might be saved! The God of the Book loved us so much that He gave His Son to die on the cross just for you and me.

God Is On Your Side, God Is On Your Side. Yes, we have trials and tribulations, but the Bible says that I have never seen the righteous forsaken or their seed out begging for bread. When we go through those trials and tribulations, we win victory, because God is on our side. If you had stopped me at some points in my life, you would have said, "Look at that failure!" Especially after I had sinned. If you had seen me at some low points in my life, you probably would have thrown me in Hell yourself! But, thank God, He wasn't finished with me yet. God wasn't finished with me. He was still working in me, and He brought me through that valley. I may not be the best thing in the world, but I am not what I used to be!

1 Samuel 30:3-6

As we encounter David, David had a problem. He was staying among the Philistines, the enemy with King Achish. But, because God was on his side, he was allowed to stay in his own village of Ziklag. One day after David had confronted Saul, he returned to the land of the Philistines to prepare to go into battle against Israel. David and his men assembled in the rear behind Achish and his men. The other lords of the Philistines saw David and would not let David go into battle with them in case he became an adversary. Achish told David to gather his men and return to Ziklag. When David returned. he found that the Amalekites had invaded his village and had taken all of the women captive, including David's two wives. All of David's men were sad. They grieved for their families. But, David trusted God. He asked for the ephod and inquired of God, "Should I pursue them?" God replied, "Pursue them, you will overtake them and recover all." Along the way he encountered an Egyptian whom had been left behind. They fed him and he said as long as he was not returned to his master, he would show them where the camp was. When David encountered the Amalekites, they were eating, drinking, and dancing, etc. It is said that David came down upon them and smote them from morning to evening..or from evening to morning. Not a one survived, except for four hundred young men who jumped on their camels and fled. David recovered all, plus took their stocks and herds.

God was on their side. God is on your side.

It's All About Us!

For unto us a child is born. Unto us a son is given. And the government shall be upon his shoulder. And his name shall be called wonderful, Counsellor, the Mighty God, the everlasting Father, the Prince of Peace.

Of the increase of his government shall be no end. Upon the throne of David, and upon his kingdom to order it, and to establish it with judgement and with justice from henceforth even forever. The zeal of the Lord of hosts will perform this.

The world that we live in today is a very technological, advanced, futuristic society. Anything that we want or need is almost always available. We have cars that talk to us. We have fax machines, word processors, car phones, and now we have picture phones. Everything that we do is stored on a disc in a computer somewhere.

But amidst all of this process and high tech, we still have a major drug problem. Crime is running at intolerable levels. In some communities, you can't even go outside of your door if you don't have the right colors on.

People are homeless, clothless, and hungry.

Pornography is all around us.

But as we approached this holiday season, everywhere we look we find Santa Claus. You can look at anybody else's birthday you want and one thing that you will never find an over commercialization.

You do not find Santa, elves, snowmen, or anything else on Presidents Day, Labor Day, Fourth of July or any other day. Nor does anyone else get the credit for the occasion.

There is a movement going to now in the world and in our churches to put Jesus back into Christmas. Even though we enjoy the exchange of gifts and all the good feelings associated with this occasion, and everywhere we go, we see pictures of

Santa. Santa just doesn't have the solution for the world's problems. Santa just can't deliver.

The fact is that no matter what we try to do with Christ. We cannot escape the fact that it is all about us.

If it had not been for us, there would have been no need for Christ who was God in heaven, to reincarnate himself into human form to be Immanuel, with us God, but interpreted God with us.

But ever since our existence we have had a problem with God. We don't listen to him. We don't trust him. And for some reason we always seem to think that our way is better. That we can work it out for ourselves, but we continue to fail miserably. Our heroes continue to fall.

In life if someone who is very close to you, someone who is a part of you is having problems, first you might send advice. Then you might send some assistance depending on the situation. But if it still seems not to work out, you will go personally to see exactly what the problem is and provide a solution. That is why it was necessary for God to come to earth. We just were not able to resolve that situation ourselves. God loves us and realized that we needed help. It's all about us.

For unto us a child is given. Means that Christ was born unto us. A child born of a virgin. But unto us a son is given implies someone that already exists. So God is making a distinction between the human birth of the child and His divine gift of His Son.

He shall be called wonderful, Counsellor. Which both actually go together. It first of all means wonder or that miraculously caused by God himself. And Counsellor which is usually used in parallel with King. Which means that He will give God-like counsel of a God-like King.

For us, necessary for us and received by us. It's all about us. World situations today need a God-like counsellor. Men can't resolve their problems. The world can't resolve our problems. We need a wonderful counsellor.

The Mighty God. This no doubt explains exactly who He is. How He could be born of a virgin and how He symbolically could be called Immanuel, God with us.

The Everlasting Father, means the father of eternity. It's nice down here to have a father. But when you have God as your father, you have a God that is eternal. The government of Christ is going to seat a ruler who is eternal.

The Prince of Peace. Instead of being a waring God which would be God against us. He came as a Prince of Peace. His reign will be characterized as a reign of peace on this earth. That is why the angels said over that hill in Bethlehem, "Glory to God in the highest and on earth peace, goodwill towards men."

But this Christmas I want you to realize that this whole Christmas celebration is all about us. Christ was born... for us. He grew up, walked among men, healed the sick for us. Opened up blind eyes... for us. Delivered the captives for us. Cast our demons for us. Healed withered hands for us. Healed leprosy for us. Raised the dead for us. Calmed the raging sea for us. Preached the Word for us. Was betrayed by us. But accepted it for us. He was tried for us. Mocked for us. Beaten for us. Forced to carry an old rugged cross up an old rugged hill for us. His garments were parted for us. He was crucified for us. He laid down his life for us. And He picked it up again for us. Because He promised us that one day He was coming back again to take us to a place that He has prepared for us. A place that has nothing but mansions. Sunshine all the time. Singing all the time. Rejoicing all the time. And you will be able to run down streets of gold. It's all about us.

Rev. John Motley, III
Christmas, First Baptist Church 1992

The Lord Needs You!

Matthew 9:37-38

In the world today, unemployment is a big issue. In our area especially, mills have shut down. Computerization has come in and we have found ourselves with a lot of what we call, "Displaced workers." This meaning that we have a lot of people desirous of the work, but unskilled to do the work that is available. So, we have a situation where there is plenty of work, but not enough skilled people in that particular area to do the work. Now, we know that regardless of the economic situation that there is always work to do somewhere.

Sometimes, we do not want to do the work because we are not happy with the compensation. That is why we have a hard time in the church getting the work done, because we do not feel that we are getting immediate compensation. But, we are compensated every day whether we work in God's vineyard or not. God woke you up this morning, enabled you to put your feet on the ground, gave you, once again a reasonable portion of health and strength, and protected you while you were asleep last night. God goes with you everywhere that you go during your day. He's the only one who sticks closer than a brother. The Lord needs you. You've been compensated.

There is always work to do in the church. But often times, the pastor finds himself carrying the load. Everyone doesn't like to go into the highways and byways. It is good to come to church on Sunday morning, put on your fancy clothes, and go out so that you can be seen. But, it is another matter to go to the hospital and visit someone who is terminally ill, or to go by someone's house who is down and offer a kind word of encouragement, or to go to the prisons to visit someone who is captive. The Lord needs you to work in His vineyard.

Christ found himself in much the same predicament as we are today. Christ went everywhere, to all the cities and the villages, teaching in their synagogues, preaching the Gospel of the Kingdom, and healing every sickness and disease among the people. Christ was not like some of us today. He did not just go to the big churches or to the places that He could be seen and get the most recognition. Christ went into the villages and the small cities. He taught them. He preached to them the good tidings. He healed them of all diseases. The Bible says that when Christ looked out and saw the multitudes, He was moved with compassion on them because they fainted. They were scattered abroad as sheep having no shepherd. Christ was moved because the people were many and they wanted to hear the good news, but they were faint, meaning that they were spiritually weak and distressed. The Pharisees and Sadducees were not teaching them proper doctrine. They burdened them with tradition of the elders. They misinstructed them. They were not taught the Divine Law. Therefore, they were faint! Souls faint when there are trials and tribulations to go through, temptations to be resisted, afflictions to be borne, and they are not nourished with the Word of God, and no one to teach them. The Lord needs you to work in His vineyard.

Then saith He unto His disciples, "The harvest truly is plentiful, but the laborers are few." There were plenty of people who wanted to be saved, who wanted to hear the good tidings, who wanted to do God's will. But, there were not enough good shepherds to go out and work to harvest them. So, Jesus instructed them to pray that the Lord of the harvest sends forth laborers into His harvest. Then, He called unto Him, His twelve disciples and made them apostles, to have power over unclean spirits, cast them out, to heal all manner of sickness and disease, and to preach and teach. Be careful what you pray for, Because if you pray for the Lord to send someone, that someone might be you! The Lord needs you to work in His vineyard.

I'm praying today that the Lord will send willing workers into His vineyard. I'm praying today that God will send them into the cities and the villages, large or small, that they will have power over the unclean spirits, that they will be able to cure sickness and disease. I'm glad today that God saved me, that He ordained me, that His spirit told me to preach the Gospel to the poor, to heal the broken hearted, to preach deliverance to the captives, restore sight to the blind, to set at liberty, them that are bruised and to preach the acceptable year of the Lord.

The Lord needs you!

How Shall I Render Thanksgiving Unto God For All These Benefits?

Psalm 116:12

We are fastly approaching the Thanksgiving Holiday Season. It is an unusual day of national observance. With the exception of Christmas, it is welcomed with a larger degree of family participation than any of our other holidays. There are family reunions, churches gather together and the entire nation takes time to stop and say thanks. Even though we say we are one nation under God, indivisible, we are in fact an entire creation under God indivisible!

Webster says that the word indivisible means; that which cannot be divided, separated, or broken. As beautiful as it sounds, it is a shame that we don't render that attitude in service! Thanksgiving is also unique because it's not somebody's birthday, or a political day, or celebration of a war that was won. It is a day set apart to consecrate the most precious things in life and to give thanks to God, from whom all blessings flow! A very wise man once said that there are only two types of people; those who take things for granted and those who take things for gratitude.

There was a story about a man who lived in Napoleon's time and by an accidental remark, offended the emperor. He was cast into prison. He was cast into the dungeon to die because of a remark that he had made by accident. As the days and months slowly passed him by, he began to lose his faith in God and he wrote on the wall of the dungeon out of rebellious anger, "All things come by chance!" He said this because of the injustice that had come his way by chance. As the days went on, he became more bitter. Then one day he noticed one spot in the cell where a single ray of light began to come in. Then in a couple of days he noticed a tiny green leaf breaking through the floor of

99

his cell. It was something that was living and reaching out toward that ray of light. He began to nurture it and to care for it. Then, one day a big beautiful purple flower appeared. His thoughts again, began to return toward God. He got up off the floor and scratched out what he had written and in its place wrote, "He who made all things is God!" Well, word got out to Napoleon's wife, Josephine, who was moved by the story. She went to Napoleon and had the man released. She said that anyone who could care for a flower like that could not be a hardened criminal. So, the man was set free! But before he left, he dug up his plant and put it in a pot with this verse, "If God so clothes the grass of the field, which today and tomorrow is cast into the oven, will He not much more clothe you?"

Thanksgiving is a time when we should put aside our illusions of independence and realize that we are dependent upon a true and living God. Consider our national blessings. There are countries where it is illegal to read the Bible. Think of our individual blessings. Think of our church blessings; free prayer, praise, worship, uncensored sermons and music. In essence, we are all charity cases. We are wards of God's never ending grace. We are God's charity cases. We are all debtors to Him. The Psalmist asks a legitimate question. "What can I render unto the Lord for all of his benefits towards me?" But before that, he says, "Gracious is the Lord, and righteous, yea our God is merciful!"

Rev. John Motley and his wife, Vicki Motley, after ordination service.

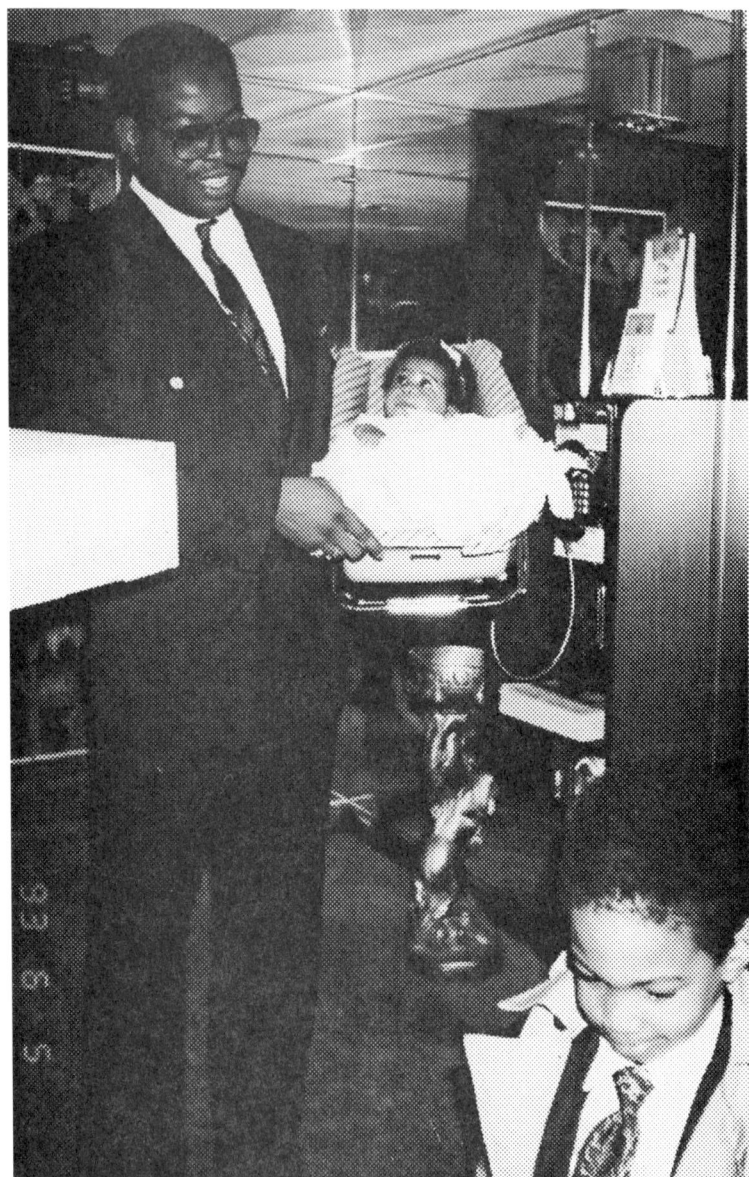

Rev. John Motley holding Imani with Sean in front at Dimperios Restaurant, Monroeville, Pennsylvania.

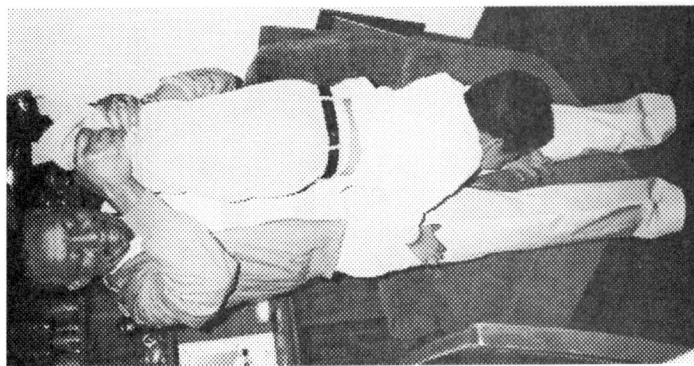

Sean being held upside down by Uncle Milton Jefferson.

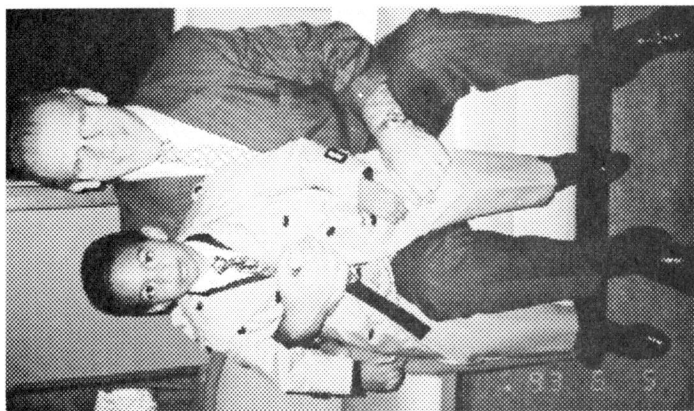

Professional Wrestler, Bruno Samartino, and Sean at Dimperios Restaurant, Monroeville, Pennsylvania.

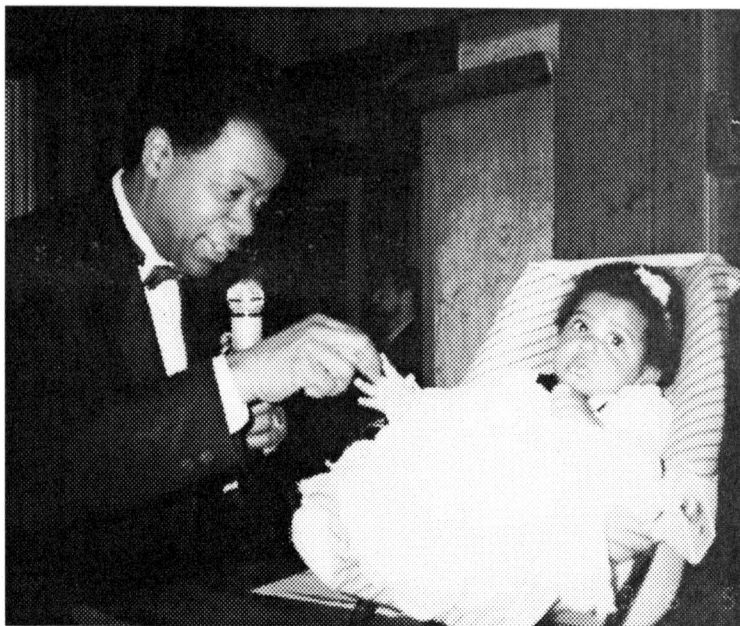

PGH singer, Walt Maddox, and Imani at Dimperios Restaurant, Monroeville, Pennsylvania.

Sean and Imani at Dimperios Restaurant, Monroeville, Pennsylvania.

Rev. Motley's wife, Vicki.

Rev. John Motley, his mother-in-law, Mildred Rue and Sean at Dimperios Restaurant, Monroeville, Pennsylvania.

(Left to Right) Kim, Julie, Lesia. (Center) Mother, Cornelia Williams.

(Front, Left to Right) My brother, Keith Motley; my mother, Mrs. Cornelia Williams and myself, Rev. John Motley (Back, Left to Right) My sisters, Lesia Motley, Julie Motley and Mrs. Kimberly Phillips

Part II
Research and Study

Free Will Versus Election

Term paper: Intro. to Theology

Dr. Spear

Composed by John W. Motley, III

Scriptural References: Ephesians 1:4-5
Romans 8:29-30

Biblical Difficulty: If God has chosen us or elected us in Him before the foundations of the world, what choice does man have in the matter? Or, does man really have the freedom of choice to accept or reject Christ? If God has chosen us, man cannot make a choice. If man does have a choice, how could God have elected us? Is there really any such thing as Free Will?

11/17/86

What About Free Will?

There has always been a question about God's sovereignty and its relationship to human freedom or free will. In Ephesians 1:4 and Romans 8:29-30, the Bible talks about God's election before the foundation of the world. This has become a problem to many people, saved and unsaved alike. Free Will is defined as the human will regarded as free from restraints, compulsions, or any antecedent conditions, freedom of decision or choice. The problem or difficulty is, if God directs everything, as stated in the Bible, how can man be a free agent and therefore morally responsible for his actions?

If God knows in advance what a man will do, what choice has the man in the matter? How much, if any, free will exists for man? These are considered difficult issues because there are many aspects that are not altogether easily defined.

111

First of all, man's will always seems to be a relatively small part of any given situation. Man has no control over where or into what family he is born, or with what abilities, disabilities, advantages or disadvantages. He is subject to many influences beyond his control. Within certain prescribed boundaries however, man does have free will. Francis Schaffer points out that when someone throws a ball to a man, he can either catch the ball or let it fall. Unless there is a physical defect, man is not so limited that he has no power to make decisions or choices.

Secondly, God's foreknowledge, which is not to be confused with His election or predestination, is not in itself the cause of what happens. Just because God knows what is going to happen, does not mean that He is making it happen. For example, God foreknew that Demas would forsake the Apostle Paul for the love of the world, but God's foreknowledge did not predispose Demas to turn back, much less compel him to do so. Demas acted freely. He made his own personal choice, under no compulsion. God also foreknew that Saul would receive Christ and become the Apostle Paul, but on the Damascus Road, Saul exercised his own free will in answering the Lord's call. We can therefore say that God knows our decisions before we make them. He knows what we will do and where we will go, but this foreknowledge does not interfere with man's complete freedom to act. This presents another difficulty referred to as an antinomy.

Antinomy, an apparent opposition of, or contradiction between two apparently reasonable principles or laws. Reconciling the two laws of divine sovereignty and human freedom is an antinomy. Both seem equally logical, reasonable and necessary. Both principles stand side by side, seemingly irreconcilable, yet both undeniable. There are cogent reasons for believing each of them. Each principle rests on clear, solid evidence, but it is a mystery to the human mind how they can be squared with each other. Each is true on its own, but it is hard to see how they can both be true together. The study of light is a good example of an antinomy as applied to physics. There is strong evidence to show that light consists of waves.

There is also equally strong evidence to show that light also consists of particles. It is not apparent to the human mind how light can be both waves and particles, but the evidence is there, so neither can be ruled out in favor of the other. Here are two seemingly incompatible positions that must be held together equally. This means both must be treated as true. So we must remain loyal to the facts.

Thirdly, does God's sovereignty in any way lessen our freedom or our privilege and responsibility to know and to do His divine will? How does this pertain to salvation? How does election fit in? Can man honestly say that God picks and chooses whom He will save? Can a man say, "If I'm elected, I'll get into Heaven and if I'm not, I won't?" If a man can say this, then where is free will? Is God's grace a part of the picture? How can we be responsible for being sinners if God gave us a hopeless start in life? How could He then condemn us? To answer these questions, we must first take a close look at sin.

Sin, according to the Bible, is at the root of our problem. Sin does not begin with overt acts, nor is it limited to them. Sinful actions proceed out of a corrupt heart and mind. We are not sinners because we sin. We sin because we are sinners. An apple tree is not an apple tree because it bears apples. It bears apples because it has the nature of an apple tree. As a man thinks in his heart, so is he and as he is, he does. (Proverbs 23:7 and Luke 6:45) Therefore, when man's heart is sinful, he will sin. "For out of the heart proceed evil thoughts, murders, adulteries, fornications, thefts, false witness, blasphemies." (Matthew 15:19) Jeremiah knew that the heart of man is "deceitful above all things and desperately wicked," (Jeremiah 17:9). God destroyed the earth with a flood because He saw that every imagination of the thoughts of his heart was only evil continually. (Genesis 6:5) The heart of man is fully set to do evil. (Ecclesiastes 8:11, 9:3) These scriptures help us to see that most importantly sin does not begin with God. Since sin does not begin with, and is not a part of Him, God in His holiness, sovereignty, and perfection, has the right, as our Creator, to handle sin, which displeases Him, as He sees fit.

Now, we must look at God's will, predestination, election and foreknowledge. The main problem confronting us is that if God chose us, His redeemed from all eternity, before the foundation of the earth (Ephesians 1:4), how can man have free will or freedom to choose his own destiny? Romans 8:29-30 states, "For whom he did foreknow, he also did predestinate to be conformed to the image of his Son, that he might be the first born among many brethren. Moreover, whom he did predestinate, them he also called; and whom he called, them he also justified; and whom he justified, them he also glorified." This is an apparent contradiction to the definition of free will. To find our solution, we must define everything that affects man's will.

God's control of the universe is often spoken of in terms of His decree. The decree of God is defined as that eternal plan by which God makes sure that all the events of the universe past, present and future, take place. To our finite minds, there appears to be many events, but with God, there is no time and everything happens in one eternal moment. This is why we say that God knows the beginning from the end. A distinction is sometimes made between the absolute decrees of God, which determine what happens, and His purpose for His creatures, that is His revelation to them of their duties. God's decrees are always accomplished, but men, through their adverse use of free will, frequently ignore and disobey God's purpose for their lives.

Another distinction is made between the direct will and the permissive will of God. His direct will is what He brings to pass. Permissive will is what He allows to happen. God permitted, but did not direct the entrance of sin into the world. Whether active by decree or passively by permission, God is sovereign over all that happens. He is under no other influence or power of anything or anyone but Himself. (Isaiah 40:13) He has the power to bring His purposes to pass. God said in John 15:16, "Ye have not chosen me, but I have chosen you, and ordained you..." This brings us to the subject of predestination.

Predestination, God's purpose for a believer that he become Christ-like, is sure to become fulfilled. Working together with predestination is foreknowledge and election. Foreknowledge is knowing in advance what will happen. Election is God's choice of certain people or groups of people to receive His grace. This choice is made according to His sovereign pleasure and not the goodness or disposition of those chosen. (John 15:16) Foreknowledge, predestination, calling, justification, and glorification are all grouped together in one package. A person who has one of them, has them all.

The sequence would seem to indicate that apart from the grace of God we cannot trust Christ. (John 6:44) We exercise our free will in the sense that once the Spirit witnesses to you, you have the freedom to choose or reject God's grace, though God through the foreknowledge of you, chose you before the foundation of the earth. (I Peter 1:2) The tragic misconception would be that God arbitrarily picks and chooses whom He wants. We do have the freedom to make a choice. God never refuses anyone that wants salvation.

Election and predestination are always to salvation, never to judgement. If we therefore determine that we do have free will, we can say that if someone does not believe Christ, he chose not to. My solution to the problem rests in I Peter 1:2 which states, "Elect according to the foreknowledge of God, the Father, through sanctification of the Spirit, unto obedience and sprinkling of the Blood of Jesus Christ." This means that even though we have free will, God through His foreknowledge elects those whom He knows in advance will respond to His Gospel positively. This in no way interferes or hinders our right or usage of our own free will.

Even though we have free will, God elected us because He knew how we would be and set us aside by the Spirit. Then, through the supreme sacrifice of the life and death of Christ, willed us into salvation. The Greek word, eklegomai, means to pick out or choose. This is a definite statement of God's elective grace concerning believers in Christ. Apart from Christ, there would have been no election and no salvation. God always deals with man in Christ, who is the one and only mediator between God and men.

In Ephesians 1:4, Paul traced salvation back to the plan of God's will, before the foundation of the world, before the projection of world order. God's choice was eternal. His plan is timeless. The fall of man was no surprise to God, and redemption was no after-thought. God provided for our salvation before one star was placed in the sky.

We must be extremely careful not to draw wrong conclusions from Romans 8:29,30 and Ephesians 1:4. God is not stating a "fatalistic" doctrine in which He arbitrarily elects some to Heaven and consigns all others to Hell. There is nothing in the scriptures about election or being chosen to go to Hell. God's election provides the means for man to exercise his own will. The Word plainly states, "For whosoever shall call upon the name of the Lord shall be saved." (Romans 10:13).

Man has a choice. He can either receive Christ or reject Him. Some men may not accept Christ but all are invited and urged to do so. "For God hath not appointed us to wrath, but to obtain salvation by our Lord Jesus Christ." (I Thessalonians 5:9) Man may accept or reject salvation from the "author of eternal salvation" (Hebrew 2:3). However, for those who reject Him, there is no escape. (Hebrew 2:3) As Luke wrote in Acts 13:26, "....whosoever among you feareth God, to you is the word of this salvation sent." No one is omitted. There is no excuse, other than rebellion, for turning a deaf ear to the gospel of salvation. No man can blame God for his condemned state for "the grace of God that bringeth salvation hath appeared to all men," to "everyone that believeth that Christ might redeem us from all iniquity and purify unto Himself a peculiar people, zealous of good works." (Titus 2:11-14; Romans 1:16)

Divine foreordination and human freedom are humanly irreconcilable, but like two parallel lines that meet in infinity, they have their solution in God. To explain this apparent difficulty by denying one or the other of these tenets is to explain away the truth.

The purpose of God's predestination was that we should experience sonship through Jesus Christ to Himself. Yes, God has made provisions for us, but we also have the freedom of choice to accept or reject Him. It is certain that man does have free will, but God, through His foreknowledge of us, knows how we will use it.

The Tabernacle

Bible Study

April 15th 1992

Exodus 25th Chapter:

The Tabernacle is a portable sanctuary that served as a place of worship for the Israelites from the time of in the wilderness until the building of the temple by Solomon.

It represented God dwelling with His people.

The Tabernacle stood in a court 150 feet long and 75 feet wide.

The sides were covered with linen curtains, which were fastened to sixty supporting pillars of bronze.

Within the court were the great altar of burnt offering and the bronze laver used by the priests for ritual ablutions. (Exodus 30:17) Ablution is the liquid used for washing in religious ceremonies.

The Tabernacle stood at the west end of the court. It was wooden structure 45 by 15 feet, divided by a heavy veil into two parts, Holy place and a Most Holy Place.

This was covered on the inside with embroidered linen tapestry and on the outside with double blankets of skins.

The Holy Place contained the table of showbread, a golden candlestick, and the altar of incense.

The Most Holy Place or the Holy of Holies, had in it only the Ark of the Covenant. The Ark was a small wooden box, covered with gold, in which were the Tablets of the Law, a pot of manna, and Aaron's rod.

The Tabernacle was set up at Sinai the beginning of the second year after leaving Egypt. (Exodus 40:2-17)

It stood at Kadesh for 35 years. It always preceded the Israelites when on the march... (Numbers 10:33-36)

Later it was stationed at Gigal, Shiloh, Nob,and Gibeon. David moved it to Jerusalem. It was set aside after the building of the temple by Solomon.

The Spiritual Significance Of The Tabernacle

1. It was a type of Christ. "The word was made flesh and tabernacled among us." Saint John 1:14.

2. Its location, entered from the camp of Judah, reminds us that Christ was born of the tribe of Judah. Rev. 5:5.

3. Its material, indestructible wood and pure gold, suggests at once His humanity and divinity. Jesus was both human and divine; God and Man. Luke 8:23.

4. The colors, white, blue, scarlet and purple appearing on the curtain and furniture, represents:

a. White	His purity
b. Blue	His heavenly character
c. Scarlet	His Sacrifice
d. Purple	His Kingly office

5. Its outward plainness in contrast to its eternal glory, represents His humiliation and His divine character.

6. Its earthly history in the wilderness life; followed by the more glorious temple, points forward to Christ's earthly humiliation and His ascension glory.

7. Jehovah manifested himself in the Tabernacle; even so, He is revealed in Jesus Christ. "The only begotten Son, which is in the bosom of the Father he hath declared him." John 1:18

8. The Tabernacle was God's meeting place with Israel. In comparison, "No man cometh unto the Father but by me." God forbids the offering of sacrifice outside the Camp or any other place except the appointed altar of the Court and Tabernacle. This was to prevent the danger of idolatrous practices and the high places which afterwards became a snare. Thus there was only one altar for all of Israel, all twelve tribes.

For us it means that there is only one approach to God and that is through the precious blood and all prevailing name of Jesus. Numbers 1:51; 3:10,38; 18:21-23; I Timothy 2:5; Romans 5:8-21.

9. The Tabernacle was a place of sacrifice, cleansing and atonement. So, "But now in Christ Jesus ye who were sometimes far off are made nigh by the blood of Christ. Ephesians 2:13.

10. The Tabernacle had inner-chambers; so, Christ has a deeper fullness for those who follow Him. "I am come that they might have life, and that they might have it more abundantly."

11. The Tabernacle preserved the law in its bosom, so Christ has kept for us that holy law. Romans 8:1-5.

The Tabernacle was a type of the Church.

1. As a type of the Church, it reminds us that in all of her teachings and ordinances, the church should be according to the pattern in the mountain. Matt 28:19-20.

2. The work of the skilled men who built the Tabernacle teaches us that God must endue us for our ministry. II Tim. 2:15; I Cor. 12:27-31; Eph. 4:11-16

Southeast view of the Tabernacle covered by its tent.

General view of the Tabernacle.

The Marriage Ceremony

As performed by Rev. John Motley, III

Marriage is an institution of divine appointment, and is commended as honorable among all men It is the most important step in life and therefore should not be entered into unadvisedly or lightly, but discretely and soberly. Instituted when God spoke the nuptial words to Adam and Eve in the Garden of Eden.

Jesus of Nazareth, honored it's celebration with his presence at the wedding in Cana of Galilee, and chose it's beautiful relations as the figure of that benign union between himself and the church. Paul, militant Missionary Apostle, commends it as a worthy institution, alike essential to social order, human efficiency, and well being. It tells the husband and the wife, to love and to be faithful to each other.

Thus the husband and the wife, forsaking all others, become one flesh, one thought, one intent, and one hope, in all concerns of the present life.

You _____ **And You** _____, having come to me signifying your desire to be formally united in marriage, and being assured that no legal, moral, or religious barriers, hinder this proper union, I command you to join your right hands, and give heed to the questions now asked of you.

_____ In taking the woman whom you hold by the right hand to be your lawful and wedded wife, I require you to promise to love and to cherish her, to honor and substain her, in sickness, as in health, in poverty as in wealth, in the bad that may darken your days, in the good that may light your ways, and to be true to her in all things, until death alone shall part you. **Do you so promise?**

_____ In taking the man whom you hold by the right hand to be your lawful and wedded husband, I require you to to promise to love and to cherish him, to honor and substain him, in sickness as in health, in poverty as in wealth, in the bad that may darken your days, in the good that may light your ways, and to be true to him in all things, until death alone shall part you. **Do you so promise?**

Then are you devoted to each other until death parts you.

Solo / Selection

From time immemorial, the ring has been used to seal important covenants, when the race was young and parliaments unknown. The great seal of the state was fixed upon a ring worn by the reigning Monarch and it's stamp was the sole sign of imperial authority. Friends o~en exchanged a ring as enduring evidence of good will. From such impressive precedents, the ring, most prized of all jewels, has come to it's loftiest prestige in the symbolic significance it vouches at the hymenal altar. Here untarnishable material and unique form, become the precious tokens of the pure and abiding qualities of the ideal marital state.

(Hand the ring to the Groom, instructing him to place it on her finger)

Do you _____ Give this ring to _____ as a token of your love for her?

Do you _____ Give this ring to _____ as a token of your love for him?

Will _____ and _____ both receive these rings as a token of your love for each other? And will you wear them as a token of your love for each other?

(The minister will now instruct the couple to rejoin their right hands, after which he will repeat the following.)

Having pledged your faith in, and love to, each other, and having sealed your marital vows by giving and receiving the rings, acting in the authority vested in me by the laws of the state of _____, and looking to Heaven for divine sanction, I now pronounce you Husband and Wife in the presence of God and theses assembled witnesses What God has joined together, let not man put asunder.

And now, may the God of peace, prosper and bless you in this new relationship, and may the grace of God abound unto you now and always, Amen.   (Salute the bride)

Prayer... (Lord's prayer)

(Ask the people to stand and receive the Bride and Groom.)

I now present to you, Mr. and Mrs. _____.

Husband and Wife exit the Church.

God Is Leading

By Jane Rhonda Walker

Dear John

God is leading
God may now be leading you
to a place where you've never been before.
Where He alone knows the battle plan
that will help your faith endure.

He does not ask you
to go where He does not lead.
So keep your victory in sight
As HIs Holy Spirit precedes...
to comfort you
to give you inner peace
even when dire circumstances
seem not to cease!

He will initiate goals
realistic to... "His plan"
that won't always coincide
with our attempts as "man".
For hope that is seen
is not hope at all.
So... rest in God and trust...
He strengthens after each fall.

No, you cannot see
where you've never been before.
But God in His... infinite timing
is sovereign... and will restore.

Love and prayers
Uncle Jimmy and Aunt Jane (Jane Rhonda Walker)
September 29, 1994   7:00 A.M.
(When I was first diagnosed with Multiple Sclerosis.)

Dealing With Multiple Sclerosis

Today is Monday, March 4, 1996. It has been 17 months since I was diagnosed with multiple sclerosis. It has taken me this long to write the final chapter in this book. All of 1994 I was in and out of the hospital. I kept having attacks and my doctor, at the time, could not figure out what it was. I am already a diabetic and they first took me from pills to insulin. I continued to have attacks.

I could not keep any food down. My body got very weak. I could hardly walk. I was in Braddock Hospital so much, I knew all the nurses on the third floor. I even found out that a nurse (Yvonne) who worked in my doctor's office also worked on the third floor in Braddock Hospital. While in the hospital, all types of specialists looked at me and checked my body. I had an M.R.I. performed. Nothing was found.

I took my family on a vacation to Virginia Beach. I could hardly walk or sign my name. I had to buy a knee brace just to walk up the street. I eventually drove. I came back to Pittsburgh. I had another attack. After being admitted into Braddock Hospital one more time, Dr. John Smith took over as my primary physician. I already knew him because he had treated me prior and was the rest of my family's physician.

He ordered a variety of tests, including a spinal tap which was performed by Dr. Mark Hospodar, a neurologist. He found protein in my spinal fluid. He wrote my doctor a letter. He said it looked like M.S. I did not know anything about M.S. A man who worked for me at a former employer had a daughter who had M.S. She had no problems walking and also no noticeable physical problems. She did have attacks. M.S.effects everyone differently. At the time I did not know that M.S. was a crippling disease, that effected most people at mid-life between the age of 40-55. I was 40 when I had my first attack.

On the third sunday in September of 1994, I preached at my home church, First Baptist Church, in W. Mifflin. I was very weak. I was, however, able to complete the sermon. Monday night about 2:00 A.M., I got up to go to the bathroom. I fell on the floor and could not get up off the floor. My wife helped me back onto the bed.

We didn't know what was wrong. She called her mother from work and let her know I would be a home. When my mother-in-law called the next morning and I could not make it to the phone, she came to the house and insisted that I call my doctor. My doctor told me to check back into the hospital. Another M.R.I. was done. This time it confirmed the condition. It was M.S.

I found myself completely paralyzed on my right side. I could not walk or get out of bed. When I wanted to move anything an arm, a leg, or anything, it would not respond. My doctor looked at me and told my wife to sign me up for disability, because it was obvious that I could not continue to work. My situation was real serious. I had gone from a person who could do almost anything, to a person who needed help doing everything. I couldn't even get a glass of water unassisted. Dr. Smith suggested that I go into rehabilitation. Someone came in to speak to me. We decided on the rehabilitation institute in the Squirrel Hill section of Pittsburgh. I was in rehab for three weeks. They taught me everything I needed to know to function at home. I remember Jeremiah, Susan, and Karen very well. We were not rich. My wife, Vicki had to continue to work. Financially, I didn't think we could make it. We were minus an entire salary, plus bonus. Even though we had signed up for disability, I had to be disabled for six months to qualify. For us, that meant April.

Family, friends, and church pitched in, and we were able to make it until April 3, 1995. God will make a way somehow, took on a new meaning. We made it. We didn't lose anything, including each other. Bills were paid, including the mortgage and utilities. Our family stayed together. We kept the same friends. My pastor and his wife (George and Avis Williams, and

126

their daughter, Leigh Tamara were always available). I did pretty well for a person who couldn't do anything for himself.

Our insurance paid for the two months therapy at home and also for the interferon 1B. The cost of that alone was $989.00. I would recommend Keystone Health Plan to anyone. By June, the legions on my brain had started to heal. Some mobility started to come back. God is good. By this time I had gone from the bed, to the wheelchair. to a walker, a series of quad canes, and to a regular cane by August.

I also started walking distances again in August without getting tired. Even though using a cane, I had also become strong enough to start driving again. I was able to pick up my son, Sean up from school again. Before I could drive again his godfather, Deacon Samuel Burrel, his uncle, Deacon Harold Jefferson, or my mother-in-law, Mrs. Mildred Rue, had to take turns picking him up from school. I and to use Access, to get him to baseball practice.

Today, I am still getting better and better. It's not as noticeable at this stage, but it is noticeable to me. God is real good. I still do not have stomach muscles. I have to pull myself up in order to get up. By the grace of God I am able to do a lot of things I used to do. I can stand upright. My balance is back, and I can walk around the house without my cane. I can also stand at the pulpit. My speech has cleared up, so I can preach again.

The most important thing that I learned from this experience is that in life, you never know what to expect, or when to expect it. In this life, one day you can be healthy and well and the next day on your back. But the most important thing is that no matter what situation you are in, God will never leave you or forsake you. My wife wanted for nothing. My children either. God uses people. He will take care of His own. People do not understand the effects of a disease like M.S. Since it effects the brain it effects your personality and all your functions. I had a two inch legion in my brain in the area that effects memory and motion. That is why I lost the ability to walk and I also had selective memory.

My memory is back almost 75% now and I'm walking better. I wanted to make sure that I shared this experience with anyone that reads this book. It is a good testimony to the power of God. Also faith. Remember, your life is the best sermon you can preach. Nothing is promised, but one thing you can depend on. No matter what obstacle comes your way, with God's help you can get through it. Hopefully, whenever your life's sermon is over, God can look at your life and say, "Well done my good and faithful servant. You've been faithful over a few things. Now I'll make you a ruler over many."

May God continue to be real in all our lives

Rev. John W. Motley, III
3/4/96

Bibliography

Orr, James A. - *A Christian View of God and the World*. New York: Charles Schribners sons, 1908.

Schaffer, Francis - *The God Who is There*. Downed Grove, Illinois: Intervarsity Press, 1968.

Laidlaw, J. - *The Bible Doctrines of Man*. Edinborough, T&T Clark, 1905.

Machew, J. C. - *The Christian View of Man*. London: Banner of Truth, 1965.

Archer, Gleason L. - *Encyclopedia of Bible Difficulties*. Michigan: Zondervan Publishing House, 1982.

Henry, Matthew - *Matthew Henry Commentary*. McLean, Virginia: McDonald Publishing Company, 1985 revised.

King James Version of Holy Bible.

Strong, A. H. - *Systematic Theology Philadelphia Judson Press*, 1907.

Packer, J. I. - *Evangelism and the Sovereignty of God*. Downers Grove, Illinois: Intervarsity Press, 1961.

Francis Schaffer also quoted B. B. Warfield - *The Inspiration and Authority of the Bible*. New York: Oxford Press 1927 used for reference.

* Also contains direct quotes and comments from the Holy Bible for Clarification.